Loss Prevention and the Small Business:
The Security Professional's Guide to
Asset Protection Strategies

Loss Prevention and the Small Business

The Security Professional's Guide to Asset Protection Strategies

J. Robert Wyman

BUTTERWORTH
HEINEMANN

Boston Oxford Auckland Johannesburg Melbourne New Delhi

 Butterworth–Heinemann supports the efforts of American Forests and
the Global ReLeaf program in its campaign for the betterment of
trees, forests, and our environment.

Library of Congress Cataloging-in-Publication Data

Wyman, J. Robert (John Robert), 1967–
    Loss prevention and the small business : the security
professional's guide to asset protection strategies / J. Robert
Wyman.
        p.   cm.
    Includes index.
    ISBN 0-7506-7162-9 (pbk. : alk. paper)
    1. Small business—Security measures.   I. Title.
HD61.5.W95   1999
    658.4'7—dc21   99-18729
                                                                              CIP

British Library Cataloguing-in-Publication Data
A catalogue record for this book is available from the British Library.
The publisher offers special discounts on bulk orders of this book.
For information, please contact:
Manager of Special Sales
Butterworth-Heinemann
225 Wildwood Avenue
Woburn, MA 01801-2041
Tel: 781-904-2500
Fax: 781-904-2620

For information on all Butterworth–Heinemann publications available, contact
our World Wide Web home page at: http://www.bh.com

10 9 8 7 6 5 4 3 2 1

Printed in the United States of America

Contents

Preface

Success is the dividend of a well-conceived rebellion. Mediocrity is the dividend of labored conformity. Every great conception, whether it be a business or an idea, was an insurgent in a world of complacency, a presence that stood in defiance of the norm and demanded attention. Yet, for some unknown reason, we refer time and time again to worn ideas and antiquated proverbs to solve our business problems.

Loss prevention is a testament to this fact. In the field of business, few aspects have remained so eternally stagnant as the effort to minimize losses. It is not the content of knowledge that fails, but the application. Loss prevention in the corporate world is an ineffective hierarchy of juxtaposing missions. The top layer creates useless programs, the middle layer creates useless audits, and those in the bottom layer numb themselves to the confusion above by searching out shoplifters in the hope of squeezing out some sense of accomplishment from their redundant duties.

No small business wants to emulate these models. The traditional loss prevention programs are an exercise of obscurity; their effect or lack thereof is diluted by the mere mass of the company. The small business has no such luxury and must consider loss prevention not as a function of business but as a component of every other function.

Loss Prevention and the Small Business: The Security Professional's Guide to Asset Protection Strategies was written to support you, the owner, manager, or security professional tasked with protecting profits, in creating strategies to deter and minimize losses in your company. The realities of liability, civil and criminal law, financial impact, work ethic, and capital investments are clearly spelled out so that you can make good business decisions regarding security functions. While investigative methods and crimes are reviewed in-depth, this is not a book on law enforcement. This is a book on business, and although we may recognize law enforcement as a needed component to our strategy, its role is supportive of the business. Every proposal and idea in this book is described in relation to one thing: the bottom line. If we lose that focus, then loss prevention is just an exercise of reactions rather than a viable component to the business plan.

Labeling a business "small" is not indicative of its size, the number of units or stores, or its sales. I consider a small business to be a measurement of vertical composition, the distance between the decision-makers and the active output. A large company may very well follow this model, and in doing so will find this book just as applicable as the one-building manufacturer. Also, a security professional is just as apt to be the owner of a store as a consultant or investigator. The lack of the position in a business does not eliminate the lack of the need. So the scope of this book is all-inclusive. That means that the financially oriented business manager may have to sit through a few pages on financial statements and the experienced investigator may have to read a few pages on interviews. What is important to keep in mind is that technique is the secondary emphasis of these sections. The relation to the business strategy is the first emphasis, so I would encourage you to read all the chapters, even if you may already be familiar with some subjects.

The fastidious observer will immediately take notice of my interchangeable use of "loss prevention" and "asset protection." When the term *asset protection* crawled out of the primordial ooze of some boardroom, the intention was to reflect a new mission statement for security, an idea of completeness in our focus and scope. *Loss prevention*, thus, was to assume a lower status, limited in its mission and application. Well, I have seen three giant companies make the ethereal shift to asset protection, and I have yet to notice anything different. So, as a matter of protest, I continue to treat the two terms as equal. Just because some folks cracked open the thesaurus and found some new words does not mean that they created a new idea.

I have strained to emphasize the reasons why programs fail as much as I have tried to suggest programs. You are the only advocate for your business, and as such you must critically assess what will and will not work. There is no such thing as a blanket formula for success. To assume there is resigns you to conformity and ensures mediocrity. The tools for your strategy are here. The success of your strategy will be the fruit of your own conception.

Acknowledgments

My sincere thanks to James Sutton, a leader in the field of loss prevention and law enforcement, for the valuable guidance and insights he has given me on business, intelligence, the law, and life, and for embracing the rebellious spirit that drives free enterprise.

Additional thanks to Steve Labbit, Costa Mesa Police Department, California. Many a cold glass has accompanied long discussions of the civil and criminal application of law. My perspective on the role of loss prevention was significantly altered by his shared wisdom and experiences.

And to the other professionals at Costa Mesa Police: Keith Davis, Doug Johnson, and Kevin Lovelady, for making the unbearable bearable and unselfishly contributing time and friendship to help me reach my goals.

And my greatest thanks to Butterworth–Heinemann for investing energy in the market of knowledge, and my editor Laurel DeWolf for investing her faith in me.

1. Courting the Small Business

When a person decides that they are no longer content serving another's ambitions and instead dives into the tumultuous arena of small business, their path to success is impeded by so many barriers that the odds of survival seem marginal at best. Consider the struggle inherent to just the first year, conceding that simply opening the doors to the business was itself a notable accomplishment. They begin with twelve months of challenges that simply were unpredictable, obstacles that arise daily as if in collusion to drive the owners back into the shackles of another's service. Supply problems, employee problems, marketing problems, equipment that fails, fickle customers, and harsh competition—the world would have excused them without judgment at anytime had the owners chosen to quit.

But they persevere. Their bookkeeping is immaculate. Their cash flow is positive and bills are paid on time. Their sales increase monthly. Their marketing efforts seem to be attracting more customers. They handle each mishap with collected enthusiasm and watch their business grow more cohesive.

At the end of the year, they tabulate the results. It's a marginal but acceptable profit. Considering the fate of most new businesses, it's amazing they ended the year with their shirts on. They are about to pop the cork on a fine bottle of champagne when an assistant enters with the year-end inventory count. The report elicits a pale blank stare. There appears to be several thousand dollars less in stock than they had expected. The conversation turns to ambiguous speculation as they carefully set aside the champagne.

Did we count wrong? Are our suppliers shorting us? Could someone actually be stealing? Is the stockroom plagued with unnaturally efficient pack rats? The inventory results offer no explanations—just the harsh declaration that their hard-earned profit has just disappeared. A line is added to the otherwise healthy profit and loss statement. In the column, they painfully scribble in red "$8,000.00." Next to it they label the destructive anomaly: *shrinkage*.

It is an almost comical term referring to unaccountable losses in any business, but the impact is anything but humorous. While large corporations are resilient enough to absorb shrinkage as an expected expense, the small business can easily be crippled by this sudden year-end loss. Worse, the process of shrinkage is so stealthy in its systematic attack that its impact is often not revealed until it is too late.

Loss prevention is the industry term for the programs that strive to reveal, deter, and control shrinkage. However, when dealing with the small business, we cannot afford to think of loss prevention as a department or a singular effort. It is a function that must be interwoven through every aspect of the business in order to be effective.

You have been prompted to create a loss prevention strategy for your small business either because you had the foresight, derived from experience or education, to recognize the inevitability of shrinkage, or you discovered the impact of shrinkage and now are striving to control it. Either way, *Loss Prevention and the Small Business* guides you not just through the doctrines of shrinkage control, but through the unique application of those doctrines in the small business.

Throughout this book, I refer to serving the needs of your client or employer. The small business owner is more often than not their own client, having to assume the roles of multiple positions, from marketing manager to human resource specialist. As such, the "security professional" does not so much refer to a person in a specific career field as it does a person with a body of knowledge and expertise. The owner may very well have to be this security professional, as may an operations manager or sales manager, or even an hourly employee. Conversely, those who make their living in security need to recognize that to be successful in the small business, they can be compartmentalized no more. They too must wear many hats, at least in insight if not in function, and recognize that they are a partner to every component of that business.

Whether you are the owner, manager, employee, or consultant, courting the small business is an affair of creativity, flexibility, and earnestness unlike any other experience. Large corporations never will demand the level of accountability that is required in the new emerging company. It is both a daunting task and a rewarding one. Here, the bottom line lies directly beneath your feet, not stories below, and the soundness of that line reflects your efficient execution of every function of your business. Loss prevention should not only protect those efforts but enhance those efforts, serving as both the guardian of profits actualized and the pathfinder of profits to come.

Creating Strategies for the Small Business

When I speak of the small business, I refer to any independent business that stands apart from a convoluted corporate structure. That business could have one small location or fifty offices scattered around a specific region. "Small" should not imply the lateral size of a company, but the vertical size, the amount of space between the decision-makers and the actual output. The multilevel corporation, with its insulation of middle management keeping the grassroots effectively out of reach from the powers-that-be, is not the model of effective business. The small business, where owners and managers create strategies based on observation rather than boardroom speculation, is the model to emulate. The status of being a small business, regardless of its output, should never be considered a starting point but an ideal to be nurtured and perpetuated. Short of that goal, success for the business is usually secured by bulk rather than quality.

This guide to loss prevention strategies was created for the small business model. It is not that these ideas do not apply to the large corporations, but that those corporations are such behemoths that the implementation would take years. The small business does not have years. Their survival depends on dynamic and timely responses to every challenge.

Whether you are the vice president of loss prevention for a small retail company, a unit loss prevention manager, or a consultant working to strengthen a number of businesses, you have a great opportunity to have an immediate impact. Working with the small business is a meaningful experience. Goal attainment can be realized and job satisfaction could never be greater. Unlike your role in the hulking faceless corporation, your actions directly affect the livelihood of people around you, and they in turn affect you. The symbiosis attained in a successful small business is the work environment most people strive for. For consultants, loss prevention for the small business is a vast market, but one that must be approached in a manner that respects the uniqueness of the people and the structures that you will deal with.

Taking a Professional Self-Inventory

Before you can concern yourself with the complexities of your client's inventory, you have to take a moment to review your own professional inventory. You bring to the table varied and unique experiences drawn from past employment and independent discovery. Every experience can potentially increase your effectiveness in this field, some by nature of direct application, some through intentional exclusion. Separating the wheat from the chaff is a difficult process. It can require not only a healthy dose of humility but, in some cases, absolution.

Often times, we mistakenly gauge our success, whether personal or professional, by measuring participation instead of achievement. Our résumés reflect an exercise in adaptation rather than true accomplishment. You do not have to bemoan this fact—your actions were a necessity of survival not an endorsement of the corporate culture—but now you are entering an environment where the realization of your goals, or the lack thereof, will not be diluted by the bureaucratic machine. You will bear nearly total accountability. Scary? Absolutely. This is why I believe that creating a loss prevention program for a small business is intensely more challenging than creating a program for big business. But, where goal attainment is at best a process of rationalization in the large company, it is a certainty in the small company, and that makes it worthwhile.

Simply put, your dedication must be to the goal at hand, not the process. Mere participation in the process will not serve as an affirmative defense to failing the ultimate goal. You may have worked hard at previous jobs, which would certainly secure longevity, but now you must work smart. The required work ethic is exponentially higher in the small business than the large business.

With that in mind, consider your background, the tools that you bring with you, and the opportunities you have for development. Most likely, you are either coming from a corporate loss prevention/security background, a public or private law enforcement background, or a business operations background. To be effective, you will need to combine and master all three domains.

Law Enforcement Backgrounds

For those from law enforcement backgrounds, you can take comfort in knowing that your experiences are relevant to the task at hand. What must be moderated is the application of those experiences, and a commitment must be made to become as apt a businessperson as you may be an investigator. Extracting dishonest associates from a company is a necessity, and a sense of accomplishment is well earned, but do not let that satisfaction induce you into complacency. Nor does an exclusive focus on shoplifting and fraud guarantee that your goal to protect profits will be actualized. It is a standard but shallow alibi for investigators to quote their arrest statistics when audits and inventories reveal huge losses. True accomplishment is reflected in alleviating losses; the statistics are incidental when the bottom line is read. You no longer are tasked to be just a good investigator—you are now expected to be an excellent businessperson as well.

When you hear of an internal investigator bragging of closing a $30,000 embezzlement case, your first question should not be "how did you catch them" but "how did you not catch them $29,000 ago." More importantly, if the lack of disciplines, a term referring to preventative and proactive programs, allowed this associate to steal this much, how many more are in the process of embezzling at that very moment? If your proactive stance can curb employee theft prior to its occurrence, then you have succeeded far beyond expectations. When you have your finger on the pulse of every aspect of the business, you will identify and neutralize the diehard thief quickly, accentuating your skills as an investigator. Your pride should be based on case turnaround, the time between the commission of the first crime and the disposition of the case. If you discover a small loss and can eliminate the cause within a few days, then you not only have demonstrated acute investigative skills, but also a keen understanding of your client's business.

One inarguable asset that you do bring to a business is your professional approach to arrest procedures. Active arrests, especially in the case of shoplifting and fraud, expose the business to the greatest liability. Detaining another human being for a suspected criminal act is a grave endeavor. Errors can result in lawsuits and even criminal charges. Looming over these concerns is the possibility of injury or even death to you, your employees, or the suspect. Your execution of command presence and control can minimize that liability. Administratively, your disposition of a case, through reports and court appearances, should reflect an expertise gained only in law enforcement.

Where you must exercise caution is in your utilization of these skills. Civil and criminal law takes on a whole new shape when concerning businesses and private citizens. You do not have the luxury of applying law to the extent that you may be used to. In addition, you must ensure that your efforts are not driven by statistics. Those who served in police departments are often conditioned to regard their arrest statistics as indicators of success. Understanding the role of police departments in the municipal structure, it makes sense that they would need to accentuate numbers to maintain funding. In the private industry, statistics mean nothing. Only the bottom line counts.

Lastly, your greatest challenge may be in effectively teaching employees even the basics of report writing and arrest procedures. You may be the foremost expert in these subjects, but if you cannot impart this knowledge to your employees, the problems associated with investigations and arrests will still prevail.

Business Operations Backgrounds

If you have embarked into loss prevention from a business operations background, you may actually have the greatest potential for overall success. Loss prevention departments often like to pretend that they are a sacred entity, but this mystique is usually cultivated as a smoke screen for inadequacies. Obviously, you will need to develop investigative techniques, but these are processes of methodology, not a secret science. If you can keep a receiving dock straight or deal with multiple accounts, both overwhelming tasks, investigative procedures will be a breeze. In addition, you have the essential knowledge of the business. Irregularities will stand out and enable you to identify causes of loss.

You will also be able to shape a loss prevention strategy symbiotic with the businesses' other concerns, because the other concerns have been yours for so long. The empathy that you have developed for sales and operations personnel will also serve you well. Your programs and ideas will complement their efforts rather than distract from them.

Corporate Loss Prevention Backgrounds

I risk sounding prejudicial every time I address the issue of corporate loss prevention, so let me qualify my statements by pointing out that these observations stem not only from personal experience, but from conversations with corporate executives from every level of the business. Some corporations may very well have dynamic and effective programs—and to them I tip my hat—but the majority do not.

Consider if a corporate executive was suddenly inspired to share his deepest thoughts following the inventory process. These are the few who have not already grown numb to the concept of critical thinking. I imagine this would be their mission statement:

> Our tenure dictates our reaction. Longevity breeds a quiet contempt for the menacing shrink numbers, and we implement a series of programs marked by clever acronyms and slogans in an attempt to harness the beast. Basically, though, we find comfort in the offsetting safety of the net margin, large enough to obscure the loss and allow us to boast success. As a matter of principle, we will bludgeon our operations managers and asset protection personnel with audits and walk-throughs, not with the hope of stemming the tide of losses, but so viable alibis can be established on each rung of the managerial chain. Blame ultimately is lost in a myriad of E-mails describing the brilliant attempts of the assumed accountable. We need only survive long enough until the next crisis diverts attention.

This is the culture of many mass corporations, behemoth vessels with strong constitutions and varied compositions that allow them to shrug off million dollar losses and continue rumbling forward year to year. The final impact is minimized by stacking the losses against the net sales, obscuring the shrinkage by way of comparison rather than action. The shareholder is adequately pacified, and the corporate giant slugs on.

A harsh profile? In the offices of any given corporation, it would certainly be viewed that way, and a flurry of compliments would ensue, each member convincing the next that the emperor is very well clothed, indeed, and no embarrassment due. Job security is the result.

These structures epitomize the idea of success measured by participation instead of achievement. Loss prevention is a standing monument to this inadequacy. It is an archaic function in most corporations, whose efforts are directed by a thick binder of outdated policies and a cyclical schedule of audits. Paying homage to the hallowed binder is a hierarchy of loss prevention managers, agents, and guards, whose strict execution of procedure is intolerant of change unless directed by the exalted leaders, too far removed from the grassroots to make effective judgments.

Large companies will employ sweeping changes to marketing and merchandising in the face of falling profits, but this guarantees only an abridged recovery, because the same effort is rarely applied to the operational core. The incessant need of executives to quantify and control every aspect of their business stands in contrast to the creative freedom that inspired success in the first place. With rapid expansion, ideas that were only applicable in their originality are duplicated over and over, and the carbon copy efforts fail to adapt to new markets and changing times. This weakness is further shackled to the growing colossus of centralized authority massing in the home office. Rather than taking the risk of empowering associates at the unit and district levels (which would require them to inspire a work force rather than control it), they impose strict programs unilaterally, as if one idea could have universal application in the world market. The more control they exercise, the more disillusioned those hard workers at the store and office levels become. With that, disillusionment becomes complacency, and this is the plight of your average corporate worker.

Now, I feel safe in administrating this harsh review because I assume that you are a qualified audience. After all, if you were captivated by the corporate life, you would not be seeking the courtship of the small business. So, if we assume the preceding indictment is true, then the next step is to extract from those years of catalepsy a useable portfolio of resources.

Don't worry; we are not going to embark upon a twelve-step program for ex-corporate executives. The sum of your knowledge is valuable; its application is the issue. Acronyms and clever slogans do not impact shrinkage. They may placate and impress nervous executives, but the bottom line has always reflected the inadequacy of these programs. The song-and-dance routines that result in affirmation in many companies will mean nothing to the small business owner when the results are not there. You must extract wisdom from your corporate experiences. That may very well mean that you have learned what not to do as well as what to do, but either way, it is still learning.

Strategies for Strategies

When it comes down to developing a loss prevention strategy for any business, the infrastructure of that plan must be grounded in some inescapable tenets:

1. You must embrace the uniqueness of each single venue, recognizing that the merger of uncountable influences dictates the climate of each business. Your planning must be microscopic, not macroscopic.

This means that if you direct the efforts of a chain of ten stores, you view each store as an individual project, unique in both needs and contributions. Correlation between business types and categories can be used cautiously in the beginning stages, but they will not dictate your programs. A hardware store in Los Angeles is not a hardware store in Topeka, Kansas. Whatever similarity exists on a statistical level is the result of averages, and you do not want to apply an average plan.

2. You must recognize that "security," as it is traditionally viewed, is an element of a comprehensive plan, but nothing more than an element, and it can only hope to support success, not guarantee it.

3. You must welcome and advance the notion that loss prevention cannot be compartmentalized in the small business. Loss prevention fails as a department; it only succeeds when it is an integrated partner to every function of the business. Whether you are a consultant, investigator, owner, or employee, even if you are not tasked to create a total loss prevention plan, this mentality will advance your success.

4. You cannot create programs that will drown from their own weight. This is the most crucial element of program planning, and the most prevalent error in corporate planning. A sensitivity to the nuances of a business is required. People are busy. Associates have duties that are paramount in their minds, and if you cannot integrate programs into their regular working structure, they will fail. Time after time I have watched the myriad of programs, plans, and procedures crash down from the corporate summit and have marveled at the leadership's futile efforts in forcing square pegs into round holes with such a righteous insistence that they practically cultivate an atmosphere of guilt in their subordinates when the programs fail. But a program that cannot progress on its own momentum is a program doomed for failure. Once, in a conference, I heard a discussion about an employee motivation program tailored around safety and loss prevention. Most of the managers present complained that participation in the interactive program was lacking. A few of the zealous and myopic members excitedly announced their high participation rate. When the facilitator asked them how they kept such high participation, one announced that they "forced all employees to fill out the cards before getting their paychecks." Another declared that the sales managers were required to make their employees complete the surveys or "they would be marked down in their reviews." The facilitator complimented them both as I wondered at the obvious irony of a forced motivational program. Here the original and worthy goal was to motivate employees to support safety and loss prevention, but the corporate atmosphere had twisted the goal to be statistics driven. If it was truly motivating, employee participation would have been self-perpetuated. Again, success measured by participation instead of achievement is the sin of the moment.

5. Beware the seduction of quantification. In the face of a symptom, we seem quick to find comfort in quantifying the symptom rather than investigating and eliminating the cause. This is akin to counting flu victims while ignoring the virus. As we scurry to create new programs to quarantine and catalogue the hypothetical flu victims, the virus continues unabated, and, as any force of nature, flourishes and survives in spite of our expressed concern. There is an expanse of paperwork, audits, and checklists cluttering the offices of executives abroad. Some audits are necessary, but the number of audits should not indicate productivity. Program audits (not financial audits—those are a necessity) are by existence an admission of inadequacy. We audit because we do not trust that disciplines are being exercised. Disciplines are not being executed because we created programs that are contrary to the nature of the business. When audits are used as a tool, they are effective only when tailored to the working programs of an individual unit. Then, they will act as an indicator of problems outside the norm, such as fraud or theft. If they are used to enforce programs, you should be quick to question the applicability of those programs to that business. Either the programs are wrong, the business model is wrong, or the personnel are wrong. Highlighting these deficiencies weekly does not change any of the underlying problems. I know of one nationwide company whose loss prevention supervisors do nothing but audit the entire store on a continual basis. The store managers are given the results, they yell at their sales managers, and then the cycle repeats itself. Their loss figures are staggering, but they have an audit for everything from receiving to janitorial. They achieve nothing, but they all get to claim participation. (Is that point getting across?) Use program audits as a tool not to perpetuate a program, but to regulate its applicability.

The Philosophy of Shrinkage

A philosophy may very well evoke images of toga-clad intellectuals discussing such ambiguous concerns as the meaning of life or the nature of the universe. It may not seem an applicable term to describe what should be a concrete financial factor such as shrinkage, the appropriate name for unaccountable inventory and profit loss.

We often delude ourselves into believing that all aspects of a business can be quantified and assessed mathematically, and that business is an absolute science, easily grasped and manipulated. As the small business develops, however, it becomes increasingly clear how subjective most aspects of the process are. Marketing may require demographic studies, but without a sense of creative instinct, those studies are mute. Merchandising may require studies of national sales trends, but without a sense of empathy for what your immediate market needs, those reports can be misleading.

The American Heritage Dictionary of the English Language defines philosophy in many ways, but my favorite definition is:

> The investigation of causes and laws underlying reality.

The reality is that shrinkage occurs, every day, by way of in-store processes, theft, and embezzlement. The investigation of the causes and laws is an exercise of philosophy and, like all philosophy, should be continually reexamined and debated. The error in corporate boardrooms is that the causes and laws are presented as absolutes so that executives can generate programs with assumed universal relevance.

Every store and business has its own reality, and with that its own unique causes and laws governing that reality. Your challenge is to reveal those causes and affect that reality directly.

This book is a tool giving you an understanding of the possibilities before you so that you may proceed well armed. It is paramount that you keep in mind that this is a resource to combat shrinkage, not a solution for eliminating shrinkage. Only your dynamic application of this and other resources will allow you to influence the haunting bottom line. From this book, you will be able to develop a solid strategy for the business to advance from. The logistics of implementing that strategy will require both networking with other professionals and hands-on training that cannot be emulated from a printed guide.

The Urgency of Loss Prevention

Over half of all new businesses fail within four years, and another thirty percent of those never see their tenth birthday. The mortality rate among small businesses is frustrating and rarely connected to the amount of effort and love of their conceivers. No matter how poetic the vision, or how motivated the founder, they die nonetheless, sad and miserable deaths at the hands of a cold and apathetic economy that will not even acknowledge their passing. Meanwhile, up the road, a huge warehouse store, despised by its employees and unloved by its owners, churns away year to year in spite of its soulless nature. How can such visionless monstrosities as that local department store succeed?

The truth is that they do not. They survive. The monster company's structure is so vast and diversified that they can afford huge mistakes. Failure at the unit level is masked by national figures and obscured by liquidation. The result is that they can quietly close a single business. The small business has neither the scope nor resources to do either. It is only in the totality of the business that the large corporations can claim success. Does this make the small venture weaker and less viable? Not at all. The worth and stability of a company is ultimately measured by one thing: net profit. But the quality of that net profit is what counts. A small business that is run efficiently and dynamically, producing a stable profit annually, is a greater success than the large corporation that has to sell off capital assets to just break even. For that matter, even a profitable company that potentially could have a greater net profit but fails in that quest should tip its hat to the small business.

Although the small business is a more righteous pursuit spiritually, the reality of economics dictates that most will fail. The shrinkage can be the final nail in a casket already constructed even before inception. So you must convince the business owner, which may very well be you, that yours is not a function of crisis intervention, but crisis cessation. Any remedial investigator can sweep in, take out a single employee case, and ride off into the sunset. You are being charged with creating a business partnership and restructuring the way an organization thinks and acts. Here is the blueprint for that restructuring.

2. The Anatomy of Shrinkage

Business owners stand in bafflement as they decipher the inventory results that report the news that somewhere, somehow, an unthinkable slice of their inventory has apparently usurped the cash register and found freedom outside the walls of their sacred enterprise. When they turn to us, they expect us to categorically define that loss and assign proportions to the causes. Unfortunately, the application of true scientific method in assessing shrinkage is an impossibility. While shrinkage effect is quantified on the bottom line, we can only offer educated guesses as to what degree each possible cause of loss contributed to the total loss. Imagine the extent of the controls that would have to be in place to methodically observe and catalog each event of loss. It would be impossible, and no one will ever be able to accurately report "40 percent shoplifting, 30 percent employee theft . . . ," and so on.

So where does this leave us as owners, security professionals, and business managers, attempting to diagnose and prescribe remedies to a multifaceted illness? It leaves us with the daunting task of fighting every possible cause with equal resolve.

Determining Assets

Every business sells either goods or services, or a combination of both. Shrinkage can occur in any business, though some have a notably higher exposure than others. Appendix B, "Asset Protection Report Card by Business," lists various business types and rates their vulnerabilities to different types of fraud and errors—it is a good guide, but again based on averages, so you must discern the individual vulnerability of your business.

Generally, you can rate the vulnerability of a business by assessing the exposure of assets. Assets include the following, all of which deserve equal protection:

- *Inventory:* All goods that will convert into sales. For retailers and wholesalers, this would be merchandise received for resale. For manufacturers, this would be parts and material. Inventory exposure is determined by who has access. If both the public and associates have access, the risk is high. Retailers such as department stores obviously have a high risk of inventory loss. A restaurant has inventory, but it is very much controlled, and thus there is less of a risk. Service businesses may have no inventory, so they have no risk. But the type of inventory also applies. A flower shop has inventory, but who except a very few strange ducks would shoplift from a flower shop? In addition, the value of inventory is important, because it directly correlates to impact on profit. The flower shop pays little for the flowers, so an occasional loss is not a risk to profit. On the other hand, a computer store has a notable investment in their inventory; even a few incidents of loss could severely impact profit.

- *Cash:* Cash is, literally, currency and coins, but we include checks and credit card transactions in this category because ultimately they convert to cash. Also, in financial statements, cash always refers to all collected receipts, not just currency. However, in loss prevention we have to recognize that each of these receipts represents different vulnerabilities. When cash is exposed to the public and associates, it is always at risk. Every step that cash takes, from the customer to the cashier, from the cashier to the safe, and from the safe to the bank, allows an intercession by greedy hands. Those businesses who deal exclusively with checks and credit, such as manufacturers or wholesalers, mail-order business or catalog businesses, have eliminated a large headache. Most businesses, though, require the transfer of cash at some point.

  All forms of cash should be considered as highly vulnerable, even in what seems like well-controlled situations. Checks and credit card losses stem from two factors: the delivery of these notes, and the systems in place to handle these notes. If the delivery is controlled, such as a service-based business that is going to know everything about their customer, then the risk is minimal. Wholesalers and manufacturers also are going to know who they are selling to, and established customers are not going to mail in fraudulent checks. If the delivery is not controlled, such as in a retail store, then the business is at great risk of fraud. Internally, the systems present to handle these transactions can expose the company to losses. As will be explained later, a crafty associate can do wonders with a credit card processing register.

- *Capital Assets:* Buildings and equipment, expected to maintain a value over time. This could include everything from computers to vehicles. Demographics of building locations could determine the risk to capital assets. Crime statistics for the immediate areas could reveal a preponderance of burglaries, vandalism, and other threats. With regard to loss prevention, our concern is not with regular degradation of assets, the usual wear and tear, but with exceptional incidents that could be deterred or controlled. Safety is a big player in this venue, a subject too broad for inclusion here.

- *Intellectual Property:* The ideas, secrets, plans, and concepts that ultimately will generate profit, or help to ensure and maintain profit. Confidential marketing strategies, for instance, would be intellectual property, as well as research and development projects at any stage. Competitive intelligence, another broad topic, would determine who or what would be interested in breaking the law to gain access to company secrets. For our purposes, we will assume that the small businesses that we deal with need a cautious umbrella of protection, but not a plan beyond the same basic physical security that would deter a burglary.
- *Associates:* The employees of a company are the most important asset and their protection is paramount. Associates cost money to train and develop. Their success translates to the business' success. Without a solid employee base, no business will survive. Some are not assets but liabilities—they deserve their own brand of attention. But most are good people who deserve a safe working environment. Safety programs are the foremost insurance against employee losses, but physical security concerns also play a role. Knowing the area's history for armed robbery, parking lot assaults, and random violence is essential.
- *Reputation:* The business' reputation drives profit, and as such must be considered an asset requiring your protection. Our greatest contribution to this end is our professionalism in handling incidents of crime and arrest, discussed at length in the upcoming chapters.
- *Customers:* Obviously, customers are an asset. Their compromise by crime or accident can affect many other assets, such as reputation, as well as threaten revenues. Our physical security plans impact them as well as the business. Again, safety plays a major role, one not to be minimized into a brief review.

In developing your loss prevention strategy, the first thing you need to do is list these assets and assess vulnerability based on research and observation. This will dictate your further assembly of a comprehensive strategy.

Categorizing Shrinkage

Next, we must be able to identify how these asset losses impact profit, and in doing so recognize the different types of shrinkage we will deal with as they relate to the business managers frame of reference. It is fundamental that we do not cultivate a private vernacular of security buzzwords and that we instead immerse ourselves in the language of business if we are to integrate into the whole of that business. No one will be impressed that you know the entire ten-code of the L.A.P.D., but they will be if you understand the difference between gross and net profit.

- *Margin Shrinkage:* Any business that distributes or sells goods works from a simple premise. They purchase goods at wholesale, sell at retail, and survive off the difference between the cost of goods and the retail price. That estimated difference is called the gross margin, the use of the term gross indicating that it is a rough figure. Businesses use this figure to forecast revenue so they can plan accordingly for expenses. This gross margin, however, is the best estimate, so invariably that margin shrinks. A manufacturer might buy one thousand units of material, anticipating good sales of a certain product. The cost of goods is set at 60¢ by their supplier, and they intend to sell each piece at $1. So they calculate that the gross margin is 40 percent of the retail price. When they fail to move that product, however, then they eventually have to mark down the retail price until it sells. The gross margin is lowered with each markdown. Clearance items at a department store are a perfect example of this model. In the end, the original calculated gross margin is the best scenario, but the gross profit is the reality. Gross profit is the actual difference between net sales and cost of goods.

  Obviously, loss prevention can do little to improve the owner's buying sense. However, monitoring the gross margin can reveal some very important insights. Loss prevention managers seem to chronically avoid involvement with gross margin issues, which is tactically a poor stance to take. After all, anything that you can do to increase profit will help minimize the impact of shrinkage. If the gross margin maintains integrity, than the gross profit is higher. What is more important is that the gross margin is a consistent and accurate gauge of the discipline of a business. The reason is that gross margin can be tightly tracked, a luxury to the loss prevention manager. Yes, the company may have had to mark down those thousand units because they did not sell. But that loss will be in black and white right before you. What if that gross margin was shrunk even smaller than the markdown would have caused? Then there is a loss issue hidden somewhere in that number. Gross margin problems usually reflect a breakdown in training or the presence of dishonest acts. Unauthorized markdowns, where employees mark down a price without permission as a favor to friends or themselves, will significantly hit the gross margin. Other markdowns may stem from sales associates working on commission making deals outside of their authority, just to close a sale. Abuse of coupons or specials would affect the gross margin. It could be something as simple as a computer error that caused a product to be sold below the intended price. Just by reviewing the gross margin reports, which most businesses generate, you could stumble upon a simple error that could have cost thousands of dollars. I have seen it happen many times, and you will be more the hero for discovering that kind of error than for harnessing a ten-dollar shoplifter. Protecting profits often means investigating the mundane as thoroughly as the interesting.

- *Capital Shrinkage:* The destruction of capital assets, such as your building or fixtures, is not something a business owner usually considers. This category does not include buying new fixtures or other investments—those are planned and intended on showing a return. Nor should you consider general wear and tear to qualify as capital shrinkage. This would include vandalism, accidents, or disasters, where insurance did not cover them. Obviously, disasters are a little out of our venue, and accidents are an issue of safety, a subject too broad to even breech in this context. Vandalism, however, and the intentional destruction of company assets, is a problem that you must deter, as well as react to if needed.

- *Controllable Shrinkage:* Some liberties have to be taken as far as nomenclature since we are dealing with all types of businesses. Commonly, straight cash theft, credit card charge losses, and bad checks are line items in most budgets since some degree of loss is expected. "Controllable" is a bit of a misnomer, but overall it indicates that proactive deterrents should minimize these types of shrinkage. "Controllable" also indicates that we can easily track the losses, which is true. Uncreative cash theft may not seem controllable, but at least you will know about it immediately. I discuss at length strategies for keeping this type of shrinkage from occurring in the following chapters.

- *Inventory Shrinkage:* This is the most volatile cause of profit loss, and the source of most of your work. This is also the only type of shrinkage that creeps up on you annually with little forewarning. It is also by far the largest source of loss. If you look at the asset categories that we have reviewed—inventory, cash, capital, intellectual, associates, reputation, and customers—all except cash and inventory can be protected with a basic campaign of common sense and physical security. These two categories, however, demand almost acrobatic feats of wonder to control. As simple as a business should be, the day-to-day complexities of conducting that business are magnified exponentially when it comes to loss prevention. The problem lies in the facts that we have already reviewed. Inventory shrinkage can only be quantified on the bottom line, and that happens once a year. That means 365 days of being in the dark. Even then, the message is convoluted, because stirred into the pot of inventory theft, bad merchandise returns, and shipping errors are the majority of your dishonest associate cases.

Maybe the inclusion of cash theft, bad checks, and credit card fraud under controllable shrinkage gave you a moment of false hope, but most of your employee thieves are just not that stupid. So when they steal cash, or ring fraudulent refunds to their credit card, or give away merchandise to a friend, they do it in a manner such that the systems in place will not immediately take note. The clever ones, for instance, will certainly steal cash, but only after voiding a legitimate cash sale. The sale is voided so the lack of cash is accounted for. But the merchandise that the legitimate customer bought has left the store. So the loss is translated into an inventory loss, not a cash loss. There are dozens of examples showing that inventory shrinkage is the most impacted by associate dishonesty.

Measuring Inventory Shrinkage

Understanding the monumental importance of inventory shrinkage, and its evasive nature, how do we work with that final number? A lot is determined by the business type and the systems in place. If you inherit a business without a suitable inventory tracking system, then you have inherited a mammoth problem. Businesses that do not use a bar code or UPC (universal product code) system for receiving and selling merchandise or material have a serious impediment in their fight against shrinkage. Since almost all manufacturers send out products with some form of a bar code on the packaging, there is really no reason not to convert the business to use this tool.

The POS (point of sale) and receiving hardware required to track inventory grow less expensive every year, and it is an investment that pays back in dividends. From the standpoint of merchandising, relying on manual counts to replenish inventory is costly and time consuming. A good inventory system allows you to track each individual product or material type, ensure timely replenishment so that customers always get what they come for, and gives you the tools not only for loss prevention purposes but for accurate financial management. Otherwise, you are just dealing with a big room full of stuff, faceless and untraceable. I cringe when I see a market or store typing prices into a standard register. As you will see in the chapters on fraud, they are inviting if not nearly permitting theft.

With that in mind, consultants and managers should have on hand the latest media on POS systems. If there is one investment that should be unilaterally pitched, it is this one.

Because the inventory process is a moot point without an inventory tracking system, we will assume for the following model that a good system is in place. The inventory process, whether for a retailer, manufacturer, or wholesaler, is a very simple concept. The enormity of the task may distract from its simplicity, but the model is elementary.

Booked inventory is all the merchandise, material, or parts that will ultimately be sold in one form or another. The booked inventory can be valued at cost, what was paid to the wholesaler, or at retail, the intended selling price. Most manufacturers would logically book material or parts at costs, since the retail value of individual components would be difficult to assess. Retailers and wholesalers could use either option depending on their accounting methods. For the sake of ease, we will assume for our model that the booked inventory is being recorded at retail value, and that the model business is a department store.

The booked inventory stands independent of other business functions. It is the on-going count of everything that has been received for conversion into sales. If you throw out an item because it was damaged, this is not deducted from booked inventory. The only adjustment to booked inventory would be when material or merchandise was shipped back to the vendor because of error or overstock. It is the true count of goods received. Capital assets, supplies, and so forth, are not part of booked inventory—they will not be converted into sales.

The *on-hand inventory* or *on-hand count* stands apart from the booked inventory. The booked inventory affects the on-hand count—when items are received and added to the booked inventory, the on-hand count is adjusted to reflect the addition of new merchandise or material—but the on-hand count has no affect on the booked inventory. The on-hand count is supposed to reflect not the number of items received but the number of items in the store or warehouse at any given time. This count is adjusted by sales and returns, and when items are missing or discarded. This system is what keeps you from telling a customer that you have an item in stock only to discover that you do not. A good inventory system would generate orders to replenish stock based on the on-hand count. Unlike the booked inventory, which provides little insight until inventory day, the on-hand count can alert you to shrinkage problems as they occur. When an associate counts a particular item and notices that the on-hand count says you have fifteen but she only finds ten, then the on-hand count is adjusted to ten so that you can replenish stock effectively. This action should also alert you to a possible loss occurring in the receiving process, or to theft issues.

Semi-annually or once a year, an actual *physical inventory* is taken. This means that every unit of salable merchandise and material in the warehouse, stockroom, and on the sales floor is counted. This is the grueling nail-biting moment when truth is revealed. Because the physical inventory is a crucial indicator of your progress, you should involve yourself as much as possible. Every item has to be accounted for and, in a sprawling building, inventory can be hidden all over the place. In addition, inventory services vary in their efficiency, and you will want to monitor their accuracy throughout the inventory process. At the end, the inventory counts for each item are translated into a value; simply put, if they counted forty circles and the circles were retailed at $1, then your value of circles is $40. The total of all the individual values is your physical inventory value.

Assuming the inventory was booked at retail value, then the total gross sales for the period are subtracted from the total booked inventory for the period. Gross sales are all of your sales without regard to discounts or other allowances. The difference between this value (booked inventory minus gross sales) and the physical inventory value is your preliminary shrinkage figure. Table 2.1 gives us the basic numbers that we will use for our model from here out.

Noting the figures in Table 2.1, your preliminary shrinkage calculations would look like this in Table 2.2.

In some cases, businesses adjust the booked inventory value to reflect discounts and adjustments to the retail sales price as items are sold. So, if you decided to sell your circles at 90¢ instead of $1, then your inventory system would adjust the recorded value of each circle sold for the new price. There is no advantage to this type of accounting over using an unadjusted booked inventory; it is just a different method depending on the systems used. In this case, though, you would subtract net sales from the adjusted booked inventory rather than gross sales. The reason is obvious: net sales are gross sales minus discounts and adjustments, so it directly reflects the subtractions made to the booked inventory. Notice this application in Table 2.3.

The sum of raw unaffected book inventory minus gross sales is the same as adjusted booked inventory minus net sales. They are just two methods with the same results. The only important point is not to mix and match; combining adjusted booked inventory with gross sales would render many errors.

Now calling this "preliminary shrinkage" indicates that changes are due, and this is where the process can get a little more complicated. In a real inventory process, some elements will be in flux at the time of the count. For instance, while the inventory was conducted, you may have been conducting sales. The discrepancy between what was counted and

Table 2.1   Figures used in model inventory process

Total Booked Inventory	Retail: $620,000
Gross Sales	Retail: $360,000
Net Sales	Retail: $356,200
Physical Inventory	Retail: $240,000

Table 2.2   Preliminary Shrinkage Worksheet

Booked Inventory (At Retail)	$620,000
Minus Gross Sales (At Retail)	($360,000)
Equals Subtotal A	$260,000
Minus Physical Inventory (At Retail)	($240,000)
Equals Total Preliminary Shrinkage	$20,000

what was sold before the count has to be balanced. In addition, some items have been returned to the supplier (or vendor, as commonly called) but the credit has not yet been received. These types of manual entries affect the value of the true shrinkage. We will assume $1,000 in manual credits and thus conclude that our shrinkage is $19,000.

Financial Statements of the Small Business

Understanding the basic financial statements of the small business is essential if you are going to instill in the owner a sense of urgency for your mission. The two primary templates used by all businesses are the Profit and Loss Statement and the Balance Sheet. The Balance Sheet shows a businesses' net worth, which includes all assets and liabilities. A Profit and Loss (P&L) Statement shows revenue and expenses for a given period. Think of the P&L as the actions of a business during any given period, and the Balance Sheet as the overall status of a business at any specific point in time.

Table 2.4 displays a typical Profit and Loss Statement for our model business at the end of the fiscal year. To keep everything tidy, we will assume that this final statement coincides with the annual inventory.

The P&L is easy to read in this format, but the larger a company grows the more accounts they add. Those accounts may have subaccounts and so on, so this simple statement can extend into a lengthy collection of entries. Usually, the P&L is issued monthly with a year-to-date column, as well as comparisons to the previous year. Any business will have the same type of entries, though a service business may not have cost of goods sold.

Table 2.3   Preliminary Shrinkage Worksheet Based on Adjusted Book Inventory

Adjusted Booked Inventory (At Retail)	$616,200
Minus Net Sales (At Retail)	($356,200)
Equals Subtotal A	$260,000
Minus Physical Inventory (At Retail)	($240,000)
Equals Total Preliminary Shrinkage	$20,000

Table 2.4   Profit and Loss Statement for Model Business

Profit and Loss Statement
ShrinkFree Co.
Fiscal Year Ending December

INCOME

Gross Sales		$360,000
	Adjustments	($3,800)
Net Sales		$356,200
	Cost of Goods Sold	($252,000)
Other Income		$500
GROSS PROFIT		$104,700

EXPENDITURES

Salaries	$32,000
Equipment/Fixtures	$4,200
Delivery	$200
Office Supplies	$150
Communications	$240
Bad Debt Charge-Off	$400
Insurance	$700
Mortgage	$8,100
Interest Paid	$200
Advertising	$500
Over and Shorts	$560
Bad Checks	$750
Credit Card Charge Backs	$2,000
Store Use Markdowns	$500
Shrinkage Reserve	$5,300
TOTAL EXPENSES	$55,800

NET PROFIT BEFORE INVENTORY SHRINKAGE	$48,900
Inventory Shrink	($19,000)
Shrinkage Reserve	$5,300
Shrinkage Liability	$13,700
NET PROFIT	$35,200

Notice under the expenditures listing the entry "over and shorts." This is cash shortage, or sometimes an overage, that has not been accounted for. Usually, this stems from error or theft. Also, notice the bad checks entry and the credit card charge-back entry. I included these to demonstrate where the "controllable shrinkage" category would appear.

The total expenditures are deducted from the gross profits, and a net profit before shrinkage is produced. This is not a common practice, but if you are going to justify your existence, it is one you need to encourage. Granted, it is an oxymoron to preface profit with net, indicating finality, and then make adjustments. But the goal here is to always remind us that inventory shrinkage is not a welcome participant in our business plan, but an outsider who distracts from our net profit. So, from that net profit before shrinkage, we subtract the total inventory shrinkage, then add back in the "shrinkage reserve," a safety net included in our expense planning that will be discussed shortly, and now we have our final net profit.

These two figures, the net profit before shrinkage and the net profit after shrinkage, are the most important validation of your efforts in loss prevention. In a moment, you will see what they truly mean to the small business and why you must not follow the standard accounting procedure used in large corporations when reporting shrinkage to their stockholders.

First, however, let's examine the other common tool, the Balance Sheet. While the P&L gives a profile of a company's actions, the Balance Sheet shows its overall worth at any specific point. Table 2.5 shows a basic balance sheet for our model company. So that we can compare it to the P&L, we are going to pretend the ShrinkFree Co. did not pay any expenses or spend any income for the entire year.

A balance sheet is easily read. It may include different line items depending on your accounting needs.

Assets are any cash, inventory, buildings, or receivables that you have. In this example, we have hoarded everything, so all our assets are on-hand. Obviously, a real Balance Sheet would vary greatly from day to day as sales are made and bills are paid.

Table 2.5   Example of Balance Sheet for Model Store

Balance Sheet
ShrinkFree Co.
Fiscal Year Ending December

ASSETS		LIABILITIES	
CURRENT ASSETS:		**CURRENT LIABILITIES:**	
• Cash	$336,700	• Notes Payable	$ 60,000
• Accounts Receivable	$ 20,700	• Accounts Payable	$ 24,200
• Inventory	$240,000	• Trades Payable	$434,000
		• Accruals	$ 32,000
TOTAL CURRENT ASSETS:	$597,400		
		TOTAL CURRENT LIABILITIES:	$550,200
FIXED ASSETS:			
		LONG TERM DEBT:	
• Land/Building Value	$110,000		
• Equipment/Fixtures	$ 60,000	• Mortgage	$ 95,000
TOTAL FIXED ASSETS:	$170,000	TOTAL LONG TERM DEBT:	$ 95,000
TOTAL ASSETS:	$767,400	TOTAL LIABILITIES:	$645,200
(Current Assets plus Fixed Assets)		(Current Liabilities plus Long Term Debt)	

	Total Assets	$767,400
	Total Liabilities	$645,200
	NET WORTH	$122,200

Current Assets are assets that can be converted into cash in less then one year. In our example, they include:

- *Cash:* This would be all money that you have control and access to. This would be derived from sales or investors or other income.
- *Accounts Receivable:* This is cash that you expect to receive in less then one year from deferred billing or credit lines.
- *Inventory:* This is the stock of salable goods or materials, in this case the same amount of the physical inventory. This line on the Balance Sheet usually is adjusted by the on-hand (O-H) inventory, but when the physical count is completed, both the O-H inventory and the balance sheet are corrected.

The total of these categories equals current assets.

Fixed Assets are land, buildings, fixtures, machinery, tools, furniture, decorations, or any nonsalable item that has a value, less depreciation. You should always be honest and annually update the appraised value of your fixed assets. In this case, our land/building has an assessed value of $110,000. This is not the purchase price, but the appraised price. Our equipment is valued at $60,000.

The sum of our Current and Fixed Assets is our *Total Assets.*

Liabilities are all our debts unpaid at the moment. Bank loans, expenses, salaries, and mortgages are all included. These would include the total of debts, not the monthly bills.

Current Liabilities are any debts that will fall due within one year. They include:

- *Notes:* These are promissory notes, or other loan arrangements that have very short terms. This would represent money borrowed; American Express would be a good example of this since repayment is expected quickly. In this example, we took out a short-term loan to pay for the new equipment.
- *Accounts Payable:* These are all monies due to vendors, suppliers, and service providers. On the P&L, this is represented by the majority of the expenditures except for salaries. This category is also referred to as Trade Payables, which refers to debt owed to suppliers for merchandise or material. Because this is a static model, we are separating the two categories and putting our accumulated expenses in accounts payable and our cost of goods in trade payables. Normally, you would pay your expenses as they came, and the deduction would reflect in the cash category of assets. However, since we have paid nothing, we have to show the accrued expenses somewhere or the model would be off by thousands of dollars.
- *Accruals:* These are taxes and wages accrued against current profits but not yet due to be paid. In this case, we have paid no one, so

the entire amount reflected in the salaries line of the P&L is posted here as an accrual.

The Total Current Liabilities are the sum of these categories.

Long-Term Debt are all obligations due more that one year from the date of the Balance Sheet. Mortgages, loans, and bonds are examples. In our example, only mortgages are listed. We owe $90,000 in principal on the building. Notice that interest payments do not matter here—interest is not a liability, just a bill, and so it would reflect in the P&L, but not here.

The *total liability*, the sum of Current and Long-Term Liabilities, is then subtracted from the Total Assets. The balance is your Net Worth. This is the current value of the company. Liability plus net worth always equals the assets. This is why they call it a Balance Sheet.

Because we have chosen to accrue all debt and income for the entire fiscal year, there is some correlation between the P&L and the Balance Sheet that can easily be made. First, notice that the sum of cash and accounts receivables equals the net sales and other income on the P&L, plus $700. That extra $700 is the inventory credits that we are waiting to receive that changed our preliminary shrinkage of $20,000 to $19,000. The quick thinker just noticed a discrepancy of $300, but remember that our actual credits received will be for the cost of goods, not the retail value. So we have $700 due to us from vendors added to accounts receivable. Also, on the liabilities side, trade payables is the cost of goods in our booked inventory—in this case, we have set a 30 percent gross margin for all goods. So the trade payables is 70 percent of the retail value of booked inventory. The accruals entry in the balance sheet is the same as the salary entry in the P&L. Accounts payable equals the rest of the expenses listed on the P&L.

Notice the Net Worth of the company. You would assume that it would equal the year-end Net Profit of the company, since the Balance Sheet was frozen for a year. Where are the differences? In two simple places. If you subtract the $15,000 equity that we have in our building and subtract the gross margin of the inventory on hand, then the Net Worth is the same as the P&L Net Profit. Because the profit margin is only actualized upon sale, the P&L cannot predict the value of merchandise unsold. However, the Balance Sheet, since it lists the inventory as an asset rather than a profit, can list the unsold inventory at its fair market value (see Table 2.6).

These two tools are the cornerstones of small business management. As a security professional, you must be able to understand those tools and discuss the impact of shrinkage on the financial status of the business.

In the Balance Sheet, all losses are just part of the big picture. A bank or investor that reviews the balance sheet of a business does not

Table 2.6   How Net Worth Equals Net Profit in a Static Model

Net Worth of Company	$122,200
Subtract Building Equity	($15,000)
Subtract Gross Margin of Unsold Inventory	($72,000)
EQUALS NET WORTH/NET PROFIT	$35,200

care about shrinkage, only the net worth of that business. In this case, the majority of the company's net worth is locked up in unsold inventory, a poor position for any company. If they cannot move that inventory, than it depreciates, and with that depreciation, the net worth shrinks. The $19,000 in missing inventory would have made a nice cushion, but it is gone. The actual loss to the company is the cost of that inventory, about $13,300.

The Reality of Shrinkage Impact

Now we return to the profit and loss statement, where we examine one of the greatest smoke-and-mirrors routines of large corporations. At some point long ago, the standard was established that shrinkage dollars would be reported as a percentage of net sales. The total shrinkage was divided into net sales and this figure was used as the uniform reporting standard. There are two flaws with this system. First, its usefulness in driving programs and strategies is marginal. Furthermore, the perception created by this system minimizes the urgency of controlling shrinkage.

Take the case of our model store. Our $19,000 shrinkage would translate into about 5.3 percent of net sales. In itself, there is nothing wrong with creating this figure; it is just irrelevant. The assumption is that some uniformity would allow comparisons between business types and units within a company. This would be fine if every store netted sales of exactly $10 million, but they do not, and the comparison becomes arbitrary at this point. An erroneous aspect of measuring shrinkage as a percentage of gross sales is that the shrinkage dollars can remain stationary while the sales fluctuate, causing different shrinkage percentages unrelated to the actual losses. If we owned a drug store that had $500,000 in sales and lost $10,000 in shrinkage, we would report a 2 percent shrinkage percentage. But that loss becomes 1.7 percent if our gross sales increase to $600,000.

Conversely, if we lowered sales to $400,000 our shrinkage percentage is now 2.5 percent. That is a large variance by industry standards, but we have actually done nothing to affect the shrinkage dollars. This means that, even though we may affect the shrinkage percentage, the same losses are occurring. I am amazed at how, as a unit manager, a shrinkage of $700,000 one year would evoke hostility due to slumping sales, and a shrinkage of $800,000 the next year would go unnoticed because sales had increased. This is perhaps the strangest aspect of corporate culture that I have ever witnessed. The problem certainly did not go away; it was just whitewashed by the sales figures. A part of the defense of this standard is the belief that shrinkage dollars increase or decrease proportionate to sales. Some loose correlation can be surmised: more employees would expose you to more employee theft; more customers would expose you to more shoplifters. In a very broad sense, there is a proportionate difference between a business that nets sales of $100,000 and a business that nets sales of $10,000,000. But we are managing one business, not one hundred, and a single business is not going to see such radical shifts in sales. So inventory shrinkage numbers in a single unit are more likely to be affected by deviation in the demographics, such as the local economy or population density. Associate dishonesty seems generally unattached to the sales base, and everyone who has dealt with labor shortages knows that associate distribution is not a symmetrical process. The truth is that many stores that experience increased sales tend to maintain a ceiling of loss for years at a time. Why would they assume that they have won the battle against shrinkage just because the sales figures offset the shrinkage percentage?

The other deficiency in this standard is the perception it induces. If your boss offered you a 2 percent raise, you probably would not begin planning a trip to the Caribbean in jubilant response. Your perception of 2 percent is that it is negligible. This is the dangerous frame of mind that you flirt with when you follow in the footsteps of the large corporations by finding solace in this weak percentage. The impact and urgency of the shrinkage problem is effectively forfeited in favor of a false sense of security. Why would you spend time combating a problem that only amounted to 2 percent of your annual sales? As busy as the small business owner is, telling them that you are there to help solve a 2 percent problem will neither gain you employment nor a contract.

A Percentage of Reality

You have to administer an entirely different approach, one that requires the business owner to face the shrinkage monster head on and realistically assess the impact on their company. I sincerely doubt that any large corporation would ever do this because, frankly, it would in most cases be more of an indictment then an enlightenment. You can keep the percentage to sales number in the back of your mind so that you can present it to investors and such, but meanwhile, right up on your wall above the calendar graciously given to you by your insurance agent, you are going to have this sign to haunt you: *Shrinkage Percent to NET PROFIT.*

This is why we created the Net Profit Before Shrinkage on our P&L. Shrinkage's relationship to net sales is really extraneous to the small business. All that matters is the impact on the bottom line. In our model, the ShrinkFree Co. may shrug at a 5 percent shrinkage to net sales figure, but what that number really represents is that they lost 38 percent of their potential profit to shrinkage. Even if you ignore the loss of gross margin and minimize shrinkage by calculating only the cost of that inventory, the business still lost 27 percent of its profits to shrinkage! That kind of reality proclaims the necessity for loss prevention in the small business.

Several important processes are secured when you calculate shrinkage as a percentage of net profit. The totality of the effort of a small business comes into play. Had ShrinkFree Co. only managed to squeeze a 20 percent margin from their sales, they would have lost around $35,000 in profit. That means their net profit before shrinkage would have only been about $13,000. The shrinkage figures at cost would have put them in the red, let alone at retail. The balance sheet may look relatively healthy, but the balance sheet only pays the bills on one occasion: when bankruptcy is filed.

Can a company really find itself this susceptible to death just because of shrinkage? Absolutely. Remember the mortality rate for new businesses. Considering that a single employee can easily embezzle $19,000 from an unheeding owner, it is very likely. The fact is, ShrinkFree Co. would be devastated in real life—our model was very conservative in calculating expenses.

If this approach does not click with the owners and managers, remind them of the most basic rule. If they have a 20 percent gross margin on an item, then for every one of those items stolen, they have to sell four more just to break even. Now, ask them if they would like to pay their employees to conduct four sales that do not contribute a dime to the business.

Every type of business needs to look at their shrinkage figures in this manner. A large corporation could never report to their shareholders that they had a 10 to 20 percent loss of net profit due to shrinkage. Heads would roll, so they will continue to minimize the presence of shrinkage by clinging to their archaic systems. Net sales do not matter in the small company. Only profit. Only the bottom line. If you cannot make loss prevention the chief safeguard of that bottom line, then your relationship with the small business is a futile one.

Shrinkage Reserves

The only instance where shrinkage can relate to the net sales is in establishing a shrinkage reserve.

Recognizing the inevitability of shrinkage in their large structure, the big businesses have adopted a sound doctrine for fiscal planning by creating this reserve account. This is a good idea, one that you should direct the business owner to incorporate into their budget at an early stage. The shrinkage reserve is somewhat akin to ensuring that your tax withholding is high enough to cover the following year's tax debt. You certainly work toward a sizable refund, but at least you are covered if something goes wrong.

The shrinkage reserve is established as part of your monthly operating budget. By treating shrinkage as an expense, you protect yourself from overspending or tapping out your cash flow during the fiscal year. This is not meant to be a resignation that shrinkage is uncontrollable, but a safety net for those times when some shrinkage wins the battle.

The shrinkage reserve should be based on a percentage of net sales. Because different businesses tend toward different shrinkage levels, and because margins are notably different from one business to the next, the shrinkage reserve should be a percentage you establish after thorough review. Table 2.7 lists good starting points for shrinkage reserves, but many factors such as your location, customer count, and security features can influence your shrinkage. Accordingly, you must adjust your reserve to a safe level. In all cases, a 1 percent reserve is a good idea, even in a low-shrinkage establishment. Remember, the majority of the reserve can come back to you at year end if your asset protection strategies are effective.

In our model P&L, the shrinkage reserve fell short of the needed funds to offset the losses. That reserve was based on 1 percent of net sales. The owner has one of two choices: plan on always setting aside 5 percent of net sales to cover inventory losses, or hire you to implement strategies that lower shrinkage. The latter is the best choice.

Rolling Over Shrinkage

Many new business owners are tempted to commit the heinous sin of rolling over their shrinkage from one fiscal year to the next. In other words, upon discovering by way of inventory that they are short $25,000 in goods, they simply ignore it for the sake of the year-end net profit, allowing the shortage to roll over into the following year. Staring at a disturbing year end P&L, this may seem appealing, but this is like kiting checks between two accounts: eventually, you are going to have to pay. Maybe the owners are hoping next year will show greater sales, and with that revenue you will be able to swallow two years of inventory shrinkage. Sure, and maybe if you let that stack of chips ride on black, you will double your winnings. It is important to

Table 2.7   Shrinkage Reserve Suggested Percent of Net Sales

Automotive	3.5 percent
Books/Magazines	1.5 percent
Cards, Novelties	3.5 percent
Camera/Catalog	2.0 percent
Computers/Software	1.0 percent
Consumer Electronics	1.0 percent
Convenience Stores	1.5 percent
Department Stores	1.5 percent
Discount Stores	1.5 percent
Drug Stores	2.0 percent
Furnishings	2.0 percent
Furniture	1.0 percent
Grocery	1.5 percent
Home Center/Hardware	1.5 percent
Jewelry	8.0 percent
Liquor	1.0 percent
Manufacturing	2.0 percent
Men's Apparel	2.0 percent
Optical	1.0 percent
Other Apparel	1.5 percent
Music and Video	2.0 percent
Service Businesses	1.0 percent
Shoes	1.0 percent
Sporting Goods	2.0 percent
Toys and Hobbies	2.5 percent
Women's Apparel	2.0 percent

coach your client never to take this route. A savvy auditor will detect the discrepancy between the balance sheet and the profit and loss statements, unless they lied on the balance sheet as well. If the business has any relationship to loan guarantors, such as the Small Business Administration, banks, or investors, they are committing a crime. Shrinkage is a debt you owe yourself. Eventually, you have to pay it. The terms of repayment cannot be manipulated by you at your whim. Compounding shrinkage will bury you in the long run. Some respite can be found in the fact that the shrinkage at least is a tax write-off. If you compound that write-off over two or more years and present to the IRS a ridiculously large shortage, prepare to be audited. To them, that suggests impropriety, and they will assume you are inflating your shrinkage numbers. When they discover that the shrinkage is real, but that booked inventory for one fiscal year cannot account for the losses, you will face further legal problems. A tax year is a tax year: it's not left to your discretion to decide when to declare losses. Most importantly, how can the owner create a dynamic recovery plan when they lie to their employees and managers? Any sense of urgency will be diminished by your sweeping the problem under the carpet.

Sources of Loss

Sources of shrinkage are easy to label. Dispensing appropriate levels of blame is not as simple. We assume that little green people are not teleporting our merchandise to an intergalactic black market, but even that is a rationalized conclusion. Collectively, though, most business people recognize three primary sources of shrinkage:

- *External:* The shoplifting, bad credit cards, bad checks, fraudulent refunds, pilferage, and malicious mischief that renders stock missing or unsalable. Also, outside personnel who have access to cash and merchandise, such as truck drivers, vendors, or janitorial services. External losses can compromise each asset, though the greatest impact is on inventory. However, some external crimes specifically affect capital assets.
- *Internal:* The theft of funds and/or merchandise by employees, or the assistance of employees in facilitating external theft, such as give-aways and unauthorized markdowns. Internal losses impact inventory and cash assets the most.
- *Processes/Paperwork (Administrative):* The holes in the daily routine, POS errors, receiving errors, inventory control errors, shipment shortages, training issues, and all of the day-to-day business challenges that are not a force of fraud, but impact the bottom line none the less. Administrative losses can impact every asset.

When surveys are conducted asking business managers to rate the percentage of influence of each shrinkage source, they are at best making general guesses. The average perception hovers around 45 percent external, 40 percent internal, and 15 percent administrative. The assessment is based on external and internal cases, and usually the 15 percent administrative is just a token percentage completely unsubstantiated. One store may arrest 100 shoplifters, but be weak in internal investigations, resulting in only five internal arrests. As a force of habit the internal arrest is factored by ten, because most internals result in higher dollar recoveries then external arrests. So the store assumes that their shrinkage is composed of 30 percent internals, 60 percent externals, and 10 percent paperwork/processes. Where did the 10 percent paperwork come from? Nowhere; it would just be unsatisfactory to report that a store had no administrative problems. In this example, though, too many factors are involved to allow for a scientific approach to determining proportions of cause. For instance, the human factor influences which crimes are detected. Internal case investigation is an entirely different methodology than shoplifting apprehensions.

Furthermore, no one will ever be able to guess the actual number of shoplifters in a store per year. In addition, no one can detect every employee theft, nor detect all paperwork/process errors (if they could detect the latter, then why would it influence shrink?). The resultant percentages are so subjective that they deny plausibility. It's simply a collective perception. The question is, who cares? Does the result mean that we are going to focus 45 percent of our money and resources on shoplifters, 40 percent on internals, and 15 percent on processes? Would you ever tell your employees that they needed to use 45 percent of their abilities toward customer service, 40 percent towards product knowledge, and 15 percent towards register effectiveness? Of course not. You would expect 100 percent effort in every venue.

The same goes for shrinkage. Shrinkage is like a lump of clay: if you squeeze at any given point the clay simply displaces itself and occupies a different area. The trick to the clay is to apply equal pressure from all sides, imploding the mass until it is the most compact. It will not disappear, but it will occupy the smallest possible area and influence the least of its surroundings. Only an all-encompassing strategy will control shrinkage in the business.

3. External Crimes against Assets

Dealing with external crime is an inevitable necessity for the security professional. Retailers are most at risk, but even the smallest service business will eventually fall prey to someone else's greed. For most people, being the victim of a crime is a traumatic experience no matter how petty the act against them may be perceived by others. A degree of empathy is required when dealing with business owners and managers. Security professionals confront so much crime that they tend to grow callous toward its presence. This cold objectivity is important to maintaining both your sanity and professionalism, but we have to remind ourselves that most people require some consolation. We need to demonstrate a compassionate stance when we speak of protecting their assets. This is a challenge for most loss prevention specialists, but acting too indifferently toward the business owners' losses generates a degree of mistrust. Calm and cool is the order of the day when dealing with crime, but no one says you have to be a robot when you discuss it with the owner.

External crime can affect every asset of a business, so a zealous elimination is in order. But these situations expose the small business owner to great liability, and unlike the big corporations, there is no legal department to clean up afterwards. Juries have awarded plaintiffs millions in false arrest lawsuits, regardless of whether or not the store employees appeared to be acting in good faith. Even in legitimate arrests, lack of discretion on the part of security has resulted in judgments, as well. When external cases go bad, either from error or incompetence, most companies find themselves settling with the plaintiffs for amounts ranging from $5,000 to $50,000. As such, there must be a zero-tolerance of error when dealing with external crime, applied both to you and any employees. We must be confident that we have employed every proactive effort to deter crime, and only then, when those legitimate deterrents fail, do we enforce the laws, and only when they directly threaten the assets of the business.

The Motivations of Thieves

Crooks steal for a variety of reasons. Some actually think that the store owes them a bonus for their long-term commitment. Others really are kleptomaniacs and steal random, often worthless, items just for the thrill. Teens and children tend to steal for the rush of it, or a sense of control over their environment. Many others consider theft their primary source of income. Most are just greedy.

Overall, three motivations exist for theft and fraud:

- *Wanting:* These are the people who are classic opportunists: they see something they like and they want it, so they take it. It is not unusual for them to have cash, even credit cards. They can be extremely excessive and take large amounts. Shoplifting is generally a crime of opportunity, and most shoplifters will not have an excuse beyond "I wanted it."
- *Needing:* These are the hardest people to condemn, because they take necessities like food and medicine. They rarely have money and usually take the needed product only. This would include a mother stealing baby formula or the transient stealing a package of cigarettes. Their acts are no more excusable, but certainly less of an indictment on human nature than the merely greedy.
- *Using:* These are the professional thieves. Do not conjure up an image of well-dressed criminals attending seminars; "professional" only indicates that this is their way of life. The merchandise is irrelevant, only its ability to be converted into cash quickly matters. This could be used to buy drugs or to support a lifestyle. Professional thieves can often be the most damaging to inventory because they know the value of your stock as well as you do. The fraud crimes, such as check forgery and fraudulent credit cards, are most often conducted by these types of people. More and more, though, shoplifting is becoming the crime of choice for the entry-level professional thief.

Regardless of the reasons, one thing is consistent. Rarely if ever will you actually catch someone who is stealing for the first time. Theft is a process of confidence building, and several successful small thefts eventually grow into larger ones. This means that the shoplifter who steals a $5 item this week will probably take a $10 item next week. But no matter how crafty they believe themselves to be, whether they are caught or not comes down to one thing: Are they being watched? If they are not, they could carry a banner announcing their intentions and be just as successful as if they practiced great cunning.

Shoplifting

The art of shoplifting is by far one of the most prevalent crimes, yet it is constantly referred to in a joking manner by the general public, and all too often by the common police officer who would prefer not to spend three hours writing petty theft reports. The truth is that tens of billions of dollars are lost annually to shoplifting and that cost, of course, is passed on to the consumer. Shoplifting is rarely a standalone crime. It contributes strongly to illegal drug use and often marks the entry into more dangerous crimes such as burglary and armed robbery. As such, the cost to the community extends beyond higher price tags to effecting the quality of life that most people strive for. Experienced police officers know that this is a gateway crime and will take it seriously. For the opportunist shoplifter, this is a chance for intervention and hopefully rehabilitation. For the professional, this is a chance for incarceration.

Catching a shoplifter is as much an art as the successful commission of the crime. Learning how to identify and limit shoplifters requires a thorough knowledge of the means perceived and the methods used by the perpetrator. Like any skill, you must learn the general doctrines and then let experience enhance that knowledge. Shoplifting is a dynamic industry. You must be open to the fact that even when you have years of experience, the shoplifters will still surprise you with new and often clever tactics.

Means

Shoplifters perceive a means whenever they can establish a comfort level in a given business. Unfortunately, that comfort level varies between such extremes that you cannot stifle every perception of means. Professionals prefer a crowded, busy store. The amateur will be too nervous to function elbow to elbow with other shoppers. An oddity about shoplifters is their apparent lack of recognition of camera domes and observation mirrors. The really good ones already avoid the stores with such systems, so the ones who will plague you often have no idea these systems are in place. How this ignorance occurs, given the multitude of television shows praising CCTV (Closed Circuit Television), is a mystery of social science. The extension of this anomaly is that most cannot tell the difference between an ink tag and a sensor tag, which either scares them off or leaves them in the back fitting room with blue ink saturating their clothes. We assume that we can limit the perception of means by putting such protections in place, but the professionals just adapt their tools or mode of operation, and the amateurs are, well, too stupid to react predictably.

The only thing they consistently look for is undue attention. Thus, the same thing that boosts sales wards off theft: excellent customer service. If the potential shoplifter believes that store personnel are aloof to their presence, they feel safe to begin work. Even a pleasant greeting will drive many shoplifters away. The best way to limit means is to accentuate customer service.

Means can also be established just by the presence of key products. You need to look at your type of business and assess what is hot and what is not. In the store-by-store review guide in Appendix B, "Asset Protection Report Card by Business," some key areas are mentioned, but the demand for certain items changes constantly. Any tools, electronics devices, or popular sporting goods items should be guarded. Books, magazines, tapes and CDs, costume jewelry, Levi's jeans, or brand name athletic shoes are a constant target. While every type of item eventually finds its way into the clammy hands of a shoplifter, some items stand out. Common sense will tell you what can easily be fenced or what is in high demand. But do not assume that a popular sales item will be a popular theft item. Anything that can be concealed and has value is fair game.

Obviously, you can lock up everything in the store to limit means, and in some cases you may do just that. In Chapter 9, "Tools of the Trade," the advantages and disadvantages of the numerous shoplifting deterrents are reviewed thoroughly.

Methods

Here are a variety of techniques to remind us how creative these perpetrators can be. Anyone can shove an item under their shirt, and that still is the most popular method, but the enlightened shoplifter enjoys methods a little less ordinary.

- *Boosters:* Under a seemingly innocuous dress can be booster girdles, girdles tight enough but elastic enough to hold merchandise, or even large rubber bands. Crooks using boosters will stay to the back walls where they can look out on everyone. Some booster equipment really takes the cake, such as fake stomachs that make the shoplifter appear pregnant, but can hold a lot of merchandise. Fake arm and leg casts are common, as are the use of layered clothing to act as a booster. A pair of sweat pants with elastic ankle bands can hold a lot of merchandise when worn under a baggy pair of slacks.
- *Shopping Bags:* Though most just use these for simple concealment, some smarter crooks have lined a shopping bag with reflective foil, and then taped another bag over the foil so it could not be seen. Why? To block out the magnetic signal sent to EAS (Electronic Article Surveillance) sensors at doorways. Any business located in a mall has reckoned with the flood of shopping bags, especially during the holidays.
- *Distraction:* Near the doors, one person distracts the associate with questions or conversation. Meanwhile, the accomplice walks right out with a cart of merchandise. This is one of the smartest routines; it's quick and clean, and busy associates are not apt to notice someone casually pushing a cart out the door.
- *Fitting Rooms:* Suspects have layered clothing under their own so thick that they can hardly walk. We kindly provide them the privacy required to take their time during concealment.

- *Linings:* Some suspects use jackets with open linings that can hold an amazing amount of merchandise.
- *Shoe Switches:* Anyone who has ever worked in a shoe store has probably found their share of old, musty shoes in boxes on the shelf that once contained new athletic shoes. Walking out with shoes on is normal. Who would notice that they were not the shoes worn in?
- *Strollers:* Do not think for a moment that a mother with her infant will not rob you blind. In fact, in my experience, the largest dollar amounts in shoplifting I have seen, especially in clothing stores, have been from mothers accompanied by their children. Strollers are vestibules of concealment, and the interaction with small children allows the shoplifter to move sporadically without suspicion being aroused.
- *Backpacks and Purses:* Obviously easy to conceal items in, but also carried by many people.

Indications and Warnings of Shoplifting

Shoplifters are as diversified a group as any. They range from the very young to the very old, the very poor to the very rich. It is an equal opportunity pursuit and knows no racial, age, gender, or religious barrier. Certain characteristics of behavior, however, should prompt you to a higher level of alertness. No list is inclusive—theft can be accomplished by people in spandex if they put their minds to it, but sometimes the obvious ploy is just that: obvious.

- Looking around nervously or slyly. If the face is down but the eyes are looking up, they are up to something.
- Shoppers initially in areas that would not normally be of interest to them; for instance, a male casually on the outskirts of the Women's department. Sometimes, while assessing their surroundings, the shoplifters forget where they are.
- Shoppers dressed unseasonably, especially in large jackets or bulky shirts.
- Shoppers who seem to avoid salespeople, or on the opposite extreme, shoppers who approach and speak to many salespeople. This latter technique helps them establish a social alibi in their minds. Most people will not avoid sale associates, but will not actively engage them either.
- Shoppers who kneel down to look at merchandise.
- Shoppers carrying shopping bags from other stores, especially those that are not in the same mall or shopping center.
- Shoppers carrying mall bags dispensed by the coin-operated racks in the mall, that appear to be empty. Most shoppers buy these when they begin to accumulate several purchases, not at the beginning.

- Shoppers with strollers that seem excessive or have many cubby-holes or a large diaper bag.
- Shoppers who carry merchandise from one area to another unrelated area.
- Shoppers who gravitate towards and remain on the back sales floor walls.
- Shoppers who consistently set their shopping bags down at their feet.
- Shoppers who make a small purchase and ask for larger-than-needed bags.
- Shoppers who make quick selections, without regard to size or color.

Gender Roles in Shoplifting

General opinion would gravitate toward the idea that men and teenagers do most of the shoplifting. This is entirely incorrect. Most of the retailers I talked to reported that their highest shrinkage areas were in women-oriented departments and that over 55 percent of their arrests were female. Females tend to take more, as well, which reflects on the different mentality they approach shoplifting with. Females tend to feel less suspected then males. Men, even as young boys, are culturally considered the troublemakers and are much more inclined to feeling watched or evaluated. Females also tend to steal a number of items: in a survey of a large active department store in southern California, over 80 percent of the female arrests included three or more stolen items. With men, 65 percent had only one item. The male shoplifter tends to target a single item, or a number of exact items, while females tend to browse and take a variety of items. Because most people, including a majority of male shoplifting agents, do not recognize that the female shoplifter is prevalent, shrinkage dollars remain high even in the wake of many apprehensions.

Remember again that no one looks like a shoplifter. If shoplifters are really successful at their life of crime, they probably dress better than you and me. This does not mean you dismiss the obvious drug addict who wanders in, but you do not limit your alertness to those people.

Proactive Deterrents

- Customer service is the key to minimizing shoplifting. Real customers will appreciate the attention; thieves will despise it.
- Try to keep your aisles in line with the registers. You want your cashiers to have a clear view of the aisles before them. Knowing that the cashiers could spot an attempted theft, many opportunists will be deterred, or at least forced into taking more suspicious measures to complete the crime. Every employee workstation should be positioned so that they are passively helping to deter theft with

their presence. The sharper employees may even spot a few potential shoplifters for you from their vantage points. This is especially important if you have tall racks and top stock.

- Try to place your clearance items along the outside walls. This way if shoplifters carry expensive items toward the walls it will be more obvious.
- Keep expensive items away from the doors. Impulse buys are usually made after the shopper has found the item they came for, so merchandise your floor from back to front rather than front to back. For instance, people usually buy jeans because they need them, so place those in the back end of the store so that they will have to walk the entire floor to get them. Jeans are high theft items and often the target of grab-and-runs (when crooks grab stacks of merchandise and run out the doors). This will maximize your product exposure as well as minimize the risk of someone running out with an armful of jeans into a waiting car.
- End-stock areas are popular places to conceal merchandise. Use convex mirrors so that they are visible from the POS stations.
- Determine if certain security devices such as ink tags or EAS would be a good investment. These systems are discussed later in the book.
- Use turnstiles or other obstacles so that customers have to leave the store by passing the POS systems. One of the appealing reasons to shoplift at large department stores is the placement of POS stations away from the doors.
- Know when to display models and when to display merchandise. Clothing obviously would have to be out in abundance to sell, but cameras or cell phones could be displayed in glass cases.
- Know the stores around you. If someone enters with a bag from a store far from the immediate area, then you probably have a thief on your hands.
- Use appropriate size bags to bag merchandise. Bags that are translucent are a great investment, as well as noisy bags. Stapling the receipt and bag closed is a good habit if appropriate for your business.
- For smaller stores, use a chime on the door to alert you when someone enters. This is very disconcerting for a potential thief and a necessary tool if you have a small staff.
- Control your fitting rooms. If you have a high volume of clothing sales, invest in fitting room attendants. They will save you ten times their salaries. Use locked fitting rooms if you can. Try to use doors where there is a small gap at the bottom. This will not distract from their privacy but it will allow you to watch their feet and see if five pairs of pants are put on sequentially. Limit the fitting rooms to three garments each. Keep the fitting rooms clear of clothing and loose tags.
- Use glass cases whenever it will not affect sales. In stores like toy and hobby stores, merchandise small to large items from front to

back. Keep the small items up front and watch for those who carry them away.

- Liquor, cigarettes, film, and batteries are good examples of small items that should be kept at the registers or locked up. No one impulse buys cigarettes, so keeping them in a locked case is important. You may have a number of items that are similar to these.

Check Fraud

Bad checks will not affect your inventory shrinkage, because the sale is accounted for, but the loss is the same to the bottom line. Though criminal laws exist everywhere condemning bad check writers, more and more it is becoming impossible to enforce those laws. Some police departments will not even respond to a bad check case even if the account is closed. Unfortunately, stupidity has become an effective defense for bad check writers and there is little immediate legal recourse for the victim. To make things worse, federal banking laws make it impossible to gain even basic information from banks about an account. So even in jurisdictions where bad checks are prosecuted, you will not be able to establish the cause you need to effect a citizen's arrest.

Means

- Check forgers and counterfeiters will perceive a means whenever they see a lack of electronic systems in place protecting the merchant. Often times, just the presence of strict check acceptance policies and electronic review of checks or identification numbers will dissuade the check forger from trying at your store.
- Bad check writers, those with nonsufficient funds or closed accounts, also cringe at the sight of electronic systems. They know that either their identification or checking account will be flagged by those systems.

Methods

To understand methods of check fraud, you have to understand the composition of a check. You could actually scribble your account number on a napkin, write "Pay to the order of," sign it, and have a document as legal as a check. Fortunately, you may accept and deny checks at your discretion regardless of your reasons. So you cannot be compelled to accept the napkin as payment. This allows you to establish check acceptance procedures as you see fit, and no one can challenge your criteria.

There are two things you are guarding against: (1) checks that have nonsufficient funds, and (2) fraud checks. Nonsufficient funds and closed accounts are academic; there is no art to the method of this crime. Forgeries and counterfeits, however, require a technical awareness to detect.

Figure 3.1 is a sample of a personal check. You and any associates accepting checks have to be intimately knowledgeable of the components of the check if you are going to detect fraud. Point by point, these items need to be included in your check approval procedures if associates are allowed to take checks. Counterfeit checks will usually be in error on one or more of these features:

As important as knowing the composition of a good check is knowing the composition of a good driver's license or identification card. Since every state varies, you will need to study valid cards and learn to identify fakes on your own.

Proactive Deterrents

Prevention is the sole key to protecting yourself from bad check losses. Some small businesses refuse checks altogether, but limiting modes of purchase isn't conducive to increasing sales. There are other ways to fight check losses without limiting the legitimate customers who prefer using checks.

Check Systems

- *Banks:* You can still call most banks for funds verifications, but many are requiring you to call 900 numbers for the service, which may be cost prohibitive. Have a list of all the banks' merchant check verification numbers available at the register stations as well as in your office. Always enter an amount higher than the check amount—you must assume that some other check is pending and if it is that tight of a margin, you should take a closer look at the check.
- *Shared Information Networks:* These systems usually tie into your POS register or into a touch dial pad. They network many merchants together so that if a check is bounced at one store, all other participants will be alerted. Shared Networks like SCAN (Shared Check Authorization Network) use both the driver's license number and the account to track the check writer. It does not mean that the check you receive will not bounce, just that it has not bounced yet. They can expose the chronic bad check writers as well as fraudulent accounts.
- *Check Guarantors:* This type of system has just emerged in the last decade. You pay a small dividend on every check you accept

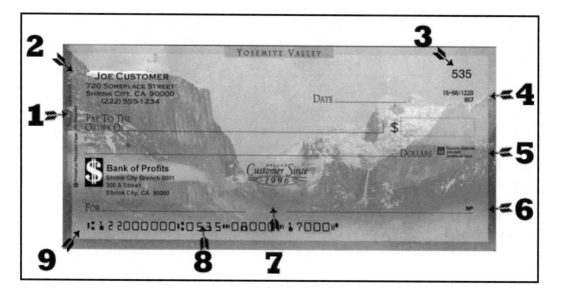

1. *Check Body:* The check should have a perforation on one or more sides. Most checks will display the word VOID if photocopied, even on a color printer. Print should be crisp and clear.

2. *The Name/Address Imprint:* This should be factory printed, not typed or stamped. Checks without this are starter checks. Be wary of excepting these checks as the accounts are brand new. Note the city and make sure it is at least in the same metropolitan area as the bank branch.

3. *Check Number:* The check number will give you some feel for how established the account is. Low check numbers mean a newer account. Also, checks can start at 1000 for new accounts if the customer requests. Some banks will issue checks at any number, though, so this is not always a sure safeguard.

4. *Routing Indicators:* Many checks will have small type near the check number. This type can indicate many things, such as when the account was opened or other bank information. Usually, though, you will see the Federal Reserve Bank routing code among these numbers. In this case, the routing code is "1220." This should match the routing code specified in element 9 below.

5. *Security Features:* When you see this symbol, it indicates that there are additional security features, such as watermarks or microprint, listed on the back of the check.

6. *Microprint:* When "MP" is stamped near the signature line, it indicates that the line itself is "microprint," meaning that the line is actually composed of very small type that is readable under magnification. When photocopied, this microprint line will appear as a dotted line instead of legible words.

7. *Customer Since Logo:* Many banks now mark the check with a notice as to the customer's tenure with that bank. Customers who have had a relationship for many years with a bank are obviously less of a concern than those who just opened an account last week.

8. *MICR Numbers:* Magnetic Ink Character Recognition (MICR) numbers are never glossy but dull. If they are generated on a laser printer they will appear glossy. The order of account number and check number after the routing code varies from bank to bank. Make sure the dollar amount is not printed down here to the right of the routing code. The bank adds that after the check is processed. Some people will try to bleach out and reuse a check that was thrown away.

9. *Federal Reserve Bank routing code:* This number designates the federal reserve district and bank routing code. Counterfeiters will use federal reserve numbers from the furthest reserve bank to allow a longer float period before the checks are processed. The Federal Reserve Bank number is the first two digits. San Francisco, for instance, is 12. Checks from banks on the West Coast have this routing number. Credit unions and federal savings and loans follow the "Plus Twenty" rule, so credit unions on the West Coast use the number 32 instead of 12. Look at your own local check to determine your Federal Reserve Bank. If the federal reserve number is not in the same area as the branch or address, than this is a definite indicator of fraud.

Figure 3.1   Elements of a Check

to the guarantor. They have bought the check from you at this point and have to pay for the check regardless if it bounces. The "pro" is that you never worry about bounced checks. The "con" is that you pay a premium for every check regardless of its ultimate status. Some systems allow you to do this check-by-check as you see fit; others are tied into the POS system and cover every check. EQUIFAX is probably the best example and most efficient company in this venue. They base their decision to accept a check on the history of the customer, previous bad checks, and the ability to confirm their information. If you have a large problem with checks, the premium for this service is certainly worth the investment.

- *Velocity Trackers:* When you expand and open new stores, these velocity programs track check use at multiple stores, alerting you when checks have been written at more that one store in a short period of time. Bad check writers often try to hit as many stores as possible in a few days before the systems like SCAN and EQUIFAX lock out their account. The Velocity Tracker will tell you that an individual was just at your store on the opposite end of town one hour ago making a $2,000 purchase. Now he is here making another large purchase. There is rarely a legitimate reason for this activity. This system also can help track refunders, those who continually bring back merchandise for cash refunds, in the same way. The velocity tracking systems can either be directly tied into the registers or can standalone like credit card authorization equipment. To utilize these systems, the associate types in the identification number and/or the checking account number of the customer. The systems tie into a common database and so when a check writer or refunder visits several stores, you are notified instantly. Either on the POS screen or on the screen of the standalone unit, you will read a message similar to "2/4/3/1460," which would translate as two stores, four transactions, in three days for a total of $1,460. This display varies but the message is the same. This example would be an obvious indicator of possible fraud.

Acceptance Policy

This is my suggestion for a sound check acceptance policy to begin with. From here you may modify as the market dictates, but even the large stores tend to stay within these parameters:

- Do not accept starter checks.
- Require a manager approval for all checks numbered under 200.
- Require a phone number from the customer.
- Checks should be preprinted, never typed.
- Require valid identification, either state or military.

- Accept checks only from those in the general area. Avoid out of town checks.
- Never accept out of state checks for any reason.

Remember that it is against the law to require a credit card in order to accept a check. The customer may offer a check guarantee card and that is their prerogative, but do not ever demand one. Identification, however, is a necessity, and if they do not have any then do not accept the check.

Train your associates to routinely write the identification number, date of expiration, telephone number, and their employee number on the check. The latter is so that you can retrain if the check comes back and the associate failed to follow your guidelines.

You may do everything perfectly and still get the check back. Most people who do not have a record of bouncing checks will pay when they receive a pleasant phone call. Others will flat out ignore you. Collection companies at this point are your best bet for recovering some, if any, of the lost funds.

In the case of fraud, the loss will never be reconciled. An example of check fraud is the person who opens an account with $3,000, then, when he receives the bank-issued checks, orders checks from a check printing company at a higher starting number. He then proceeds to write checks all over town between Friday night and Sunday night. When those merchants check the funds available via the bank, plenty of money is there supposedly to cover the check. Equifax might not accept the checks if they are queried several times in a few days on a new account, but most likely, he will write checks freely all weekend. Monday morning, he promptly removes all the cash in the checking account and leaves town. He wrote $50,000 in checks and every one of them will bounce. The irony is that in some jurisdictions, you would still have to struggle to establish that he had criminal intent and that it is not a civil matter.

Some level of loss will be seen if you accept checks. The goal is to keep check losses at a level commensurate with your shrinkage goal. I would not compare your check losses to net sales, as the large companies do, but instead try to compare check loss to the total of all checks received. Then you can compare your total checks to total sales and determine if additional systems would be a good investment.

Credit Card Fraud

People who commit fraud with credit cards are either in an organized ring or have committed other crimes such as burglary or robbery. Because a proactive defense can eliminate charge-backs, the term used when the banks charge you back the amount of the purchase, it is recommended that you do not aggressively pursue credit card fraud cases. The investigative process is delicate, and for third-party credit cards (VISA, MasterCard, American Express, or Discover—third party means that the money belongs to an outside bank, versus a card issued specifically for your business, like those obtained at most department stores) mistakes can happen often, leaving the business you represent in a liable position. Too often an angry boyfriend calls in his card as stolen to punish the girlfriend, and that is something you do not need to be involved in. Also, nothing is more embarrassing than calling the police because the person using the card is not authorized, only to find out that the person is a mistress to a married man who gave her the card. It happens more often than you would imagine. Many large retailers will not even make an apprehension on any third-party card transaction for these reasons. Whether you choose to confront credit card fraud or simply deter it is an issue to be addressed at length with your client. I would generally discourage allowing security guards or loss prevention agents to make these arrests unless they have been thoroughly trained.

Means

Credit card fraud costs us billions of dollars annually and is perhaps the most lucrative pursuit in fraud. The ramifications if the perpetrator is caught are not that stringent, even though the associated crimes are felonies in most states. Over 70 percent of credit fraud occurs during the hectic holiday season, because the greatest means of conducting fraud presents itself when time is short and associates are hurried. Time is the ally of credit fraud. When you try to compose the cause for arrest in a credit card case, you are running against the clock.

In addition to rushed sales floors facilitating this crime, the thief also will look for other avenues. Mail-order businesses can be drowned in credit fraud. Any business that accepts credit card orders over the phone is at risk. Businesses that sell high-value merchandise and do not check identification also invite these crimes.

Methods

Credit card crime may stem from an act of opportunity or an act of decisive planning. In the case of opportunity, a legitimate credit card may have been stolen from the mail, from a wallet or purse, or during the commission of a more serious crime, such as robbery. The opportunist will act quickly and nervously. They will not have matching identification, or if they do, it is the identification of the original owner of the card and even a passing look will reveal that. These thieves are nervous and excitable. They will collect as much merchandise as possible in a short time, giving little regard to sizes, colors, or other factors that regular shoppers consider. They will complain about delays in processing, but for some reason hang around long enough for you to determine that the card is stolen. When presenting identification, they will try to mask the picture with their hand. They can be very talkative, often overfriendly with the sales associate, trying to quell their sense of nervousness.

When the fraud is part of an organized effort, the entire game changes. The professional usually has access to many cards or many card numbers. They will have their own magnetic encoder so that they can change the information on the magnetic strips often. Many create their own cards, and their own banks for that matter. The assumption is that no one will take the time to notice the fine details of a credit card. Your job is to make sure every employee, as a reflex, checks those fine details.

Indications and Warnings

- Quick selection of high-dollar merchandise or quick decisions on purchasing high-end merchandise is very common, especially with the opportunist.
- The opportunist will usually produce the credit card from a pocket, or loose from their purse. They do not tend to carry them in their wallets. This may be because they do not want to prompt the associate to ask for identification or because basic psychology tends to cause them to isolate this criminal tool from their personal things.
- Commonly, the criminal will hand the stolen or forged card to the associate, then walk away as if looking at other merchandise. Most of us would never leave our card during a transaction. They do this to avoid the issue of identification and to avoid any questions.
- Anyone who says they do not have identification is immediately suspect. Ordinary people do not carry the credit cards while leaving their identification in the car or at home. I have never seen a customer say "I have to get my license from the car" and actually return with it.
- Remagnetized cards will show embossed numbers on the card different from what prints on the register. It is common for the perpetrators to use the same credit card over and over, but different account numbers. This allows them to use one false identification with the same physical card, avoiding the costs of producing numerous false IDs.
- The first five numbers of the credit card indicate the issuing bank. One quick phone call to the merchant services number of the credit card company can reveal if the account belongs to the bank named on the card.

- Many forgeries are of poor quality. The corners are squared instead of rounded. The hologram seems dull and crooked. Print is not parallel to the top and sides of the card. The numbers may appear punched out; this is an old but tried method, removing account numbers with a razor blade and gluing new ones in place. The ink may smear when rubbed, an impossibility with legitimate cards since they are heavily laminated.

Proactive Deterrents

Guarding against credit card fraud requires you to understand the financial nature of the credit card. Knowing this, you quickly discover that your business does not have to take on the daunting task of credit card investigation, but instead can eliminate losses without ever making an arrest.

The Bank/Broker Relationship

VISA and MasterCard are not owned by Visa and MasterCard. Those companies are basically large clearing houses that earn their money by taking a percentage of each sale. You pay this price for the convenience of being able to accept the card. Individual banks actually own the cards and make their money from the interest and fees. American Express does own their cards as does Discover. You deal directly with the issuing institution in these cases.

Charge-Backs

Your goal here is to avoid charge-backs, having the bank deny payment for the transaction. They can only do this when you fail to follow the procedures laid out by them for card acceptance. Charge-backs are completely avoidable, and associates should understand that their failure to properly handle credit card transactions will not be tolerated.

The most common reasons for charge-backs are that the ringing associate failed to capture a signature with the sale or that the number printed on the receipt did not match numbers on the card, detected by the banks when the name signed does not match the name on the account. The acceptance procedures vary slightly with each company, but these procedures will cover you universally and ensure that you do not have to eat the cost of credit fraud. You must ensure that every associate is taught these procedures:

- When accepting the card, do not swipe and return the card. Place the card on the register face up.
- Look at the card. Security features on credit cards are plentiful and they are difficult to forge. Some banks have more security features

than others, however, there are certain qualities universal to the respective cards. The hologram should be clear and not two-dimensional. The embossed numbers should never be flat or crooked. The first four digits of the card number should be printed on the face of the card, above or below the embossed number. The signature on the panel should have multicolored printing for Visa and MasterCard. The print around the hologram is microprint and will appear jagged if forged. Visa always has the "flying V," sort of a reverse italics letter "V" after the expiration date. MasterCard has a unique "MC" with the letter C slightly overlapping the letter M.

- After swiping the card, ensure that the number captured by the register or touch pad is the same as the number embossed on the card.
- Be watchful for Test Cards. These account numbers are used for register and computer testing and will immediately return an approval number. No real account will immediately return an approval number upon swiping. The system usually requires ten to thirty seconds to connect and exchange data.
- If the card cannot be read by the swipe, manually enter the number, but then make an imprint with a manual card imprinter.
- Capture the signature. If you use signature pads that record the signature digitally, make sure they are always working. If you cannot capture the signature electronically, have the customer sign a duplicate copy or a manual form with the card imprinted on it.
- Check the signature against the signature on the card. If there is no signature on the card, ask for identification.
- In high-risk businesses, ask for identification as a matter of policy.
- If you accept phone orders for later delivery or pick-up, you must require the customer to present their card and identification at some point. Do not let them just walk in and pick up the merchandise.
- Create a code name or other scenario that associates can use when they suspect a card is fraudulent. They should be able to call a manager or security without arousing the suspicions of the presenter. The best act is to have the associate pretend that they are calling the credit card company for approval because systems are down. If that fails, they should know to hand off the credit card number to another associate so that they can call security. This trickery requires some practice—associates should not be naturally adept at lying—so work with them as part of their training.

These are simple steps, yet merchants still swallow overwhelming losses due to charge-backs annually. As long as you have the signature captured and you compare the embossed number to the magnetic number on the POS screen or tape, then you will avoid this loss. VISA, MasterCard, American Express, and Discover all provide excellent resource material for training in fraud detection. Issuing banks will also provide you with ample posters and brochures to guide your associates.

Counterfeit Currency

In a world of electronic commerce, it is comforting that the good old green back still manages to rule supreme. As old as the institution of money itself is the art of counterfeiting. It is literally an art to duplicate the intricate design of currency, though with the advent of color copiers many amateurs have managed to infringe on this once sacred craft. At least if your business accepts a good counterfeit, you can respect the intense work required to create the misleading document. If your well-trained associates intercept the deceitful imposter, then kudos are well deserved.

Means

The artists who create plausible fake currency are not going to come into your business and push counterfeits over the transom. They use "mules" who attempt to convert the fake bills into real cash by making small purchases with big bills. Retailers are mostly the target of counterfeiters since they deal with an immense amount of cash sales. Means is perceived by the mules anytime they believe that associates are not alert, especially during the holidays and peak hours.

Methods

Counterfeits can be of exceptional quality, remaining in circulation for sometime, or they can be cursory attempts at fraud. Color photocopies and laser-printed money should stand out like a sore thumb, but they still slip through. When this kind of funny money is accepted, someone is sleeping at their post. Paste-ups, where pieces of one bill are glued to another, also are a tacky but effective way to rip off the business. Any time there is at least 50 percent of a U.S. bill intact, the banks or treasury department is required to replace that bill. So, a crook will cut the four corners of a twenty dollar bill off and glue them to the four corners on the face of a one-dollar bill. The business accepts the unique "twenty" with Washington's face on it, and the crook exchanges the defaced real twenty for a new one. It's an easy way to double your money in a short time.

Good counterfeits are hard to detect. It is somewhat like playing the child's card game "Old Maid"—everyone hopes they do not get stuck with the bad card, but eventually someone does. If the bank finds counterfeits in your deposit, they debit your account and send the counterfeits right back to you. It is the business's responsibility to make sure the money it receives is real money.

Proactive Deterrents

- Fortunately, the government is making it more and more difficult for counterfeiters. Magnetic strips, colored threads, and watermarks are the hallmarks of the new and improved bills. Of course, this is all ineffective if the associates who are handling the money do not take the time to look at it.

- Every register station should have a small, inexpensive fluorescent light below the register. This will allow the associate to quickly and inconspicuously check the watermark on twenties and hundreds. Many will not feel comfortable holding the bill up to the overhead lights, and for good reason. It is a bit insulting to the honest customer.
- Counterfeit detection pens are very inexpensive and last for a long time. They react to the paper when you mark on a bill and the resultant color indicates whether it is authentic. Counterfeiters have created some excellent artwork in their craft but no one has been successful in perfectly duplicating the paper stock used.

Traveler's Checks and Money Orders

Depending on the location and type of business, use of Traveler's Checks or money orders may be common or completely unheard of. Traveler's Checks are not to be shied away from; after all, they are usually carried by tourists and tourism can really strengthen sales. Additionally, the check issuers have installed better security features in their notes than the U.S. Government has in currency, certainly motivated by the fact that the government doesn't pay the bill for counterfeits but the check issuers do. Like credit cards, the following set of procedures will ensure that you are paid even if the check is a fraud.

Means

A business is at risk of counterfeit traveler's checks and money orders for the same reasons as counterfeit checks or credit cards, usually during peak sales times when associates are busiest.

Methods

Traveler's checks and money orders are forged in much the same fashion as counterfeit currency. Some are poor mock-ups, others sophisticated forgery. They are usually passed in exchange for high-value merchandise, or, as with currency, very small purchases in the effort to receive real money.

Proactive Deterrents

These forms of payment are secured by the issuing bank, so, when properly accepted, they are just like cash. However, they are treated by the banks with similar procedural requirements as credit cards. Fortunately, they are, regardless of the name, never treated by the bank as standard checks. Those notes are the bank's responsibility, so unlike the situation with personal checks, they will happily support your investigation with any information you need. Most of the check issuers even have toll-free lines to call just to authenticate the check numbers. So you need to welcome Traveler's Checks as cash but apply the same cautions due to credit card transactions.

- I would question the use of money orders; it is unusual to buy money orders and then go shopping. Because money orders are issued by convenience stores and other outlets in a variety of forms, be very thorough in your authentication process.
- Traveler's checks are often counterfeited, although now they have excellent security features as well. Most traveler's checks are issued by the credit card companies. The most popular are VISA and American Express traveler's checks. Look for the security features—both companies will send you check specimens as well as guides to educate you.
- Make sure that the check is countersigned in front of the accepting associate, not before.
- Unless it is a stunning counterfeit, both VISA and American Express are quick to return bad checks without payment. In my experience, though, when this happens it is because the check was a terrible facsimile. Alertness on the part of the associate is the best defense.
- If necessary, make it a policy that all traveler's checks must be called in to the issuing bank. The issuing agencies all have 800 numbers for authenticating checks. This may not be feasible if your business is in a high-tourist area, but for most businesses it is a reasonable and foolproof solution to getting stuck with the bill.

Till Tapping

Till tapping is the all-encompassing term for nonassociates stealing cash directly from the register. This is not an opportunist crime; usually, the suspect is a master at this craft, as it requires a lot of confidence and quick actions.

Means

Till tappers look for businesses where registers are far apart, such as department stores. They look for single associates in departments that are not crowded. Access is important, so registers that are on islands are a bonus. They also look for businesses that do a lot of cash sales and do not have drop-vaults, the slotted vaults built into register tables that money can routinely be dropped into.

Methods

- Some till tappers will attempt to watch and see what entries are required to open the register. Then they will request that the associate check the stock room for an obscure item and open the register while they are gone.
- The slight-of-hand method is to make a purchase, then drop something over the counter so that the associate has to bend down in the middle of a transaction, such as a credit card or driver's license. Within seconds, the cash is in their pocket.
- Many till tappers work with accomplices. They will use the accomplices to distract the associate when the cash drawer is open, or the purchaser will lead the associate from the register by asking about some item while the accomplice takes the cash.

Proactive Deterrents

- The associates must be trained in safe money handling and how till tappers operate. Most would not believe how fast these people work, and you need to emphasis the need for continual alertness.
- The register drawers should be key locked if the associate is going to be out of the area for any period of time. Using pass codes to open registers should only be allowed when someone is consistently in the area.
- Cash drop-vaults should be in place at the registers. Associates should place large bills in this vault so that they are not in the till. If this is not available, have the associate place $20 and higher denominations under the cash tray so that they are not easily accessible.
- Position registers away from the edges of the counters. You want the potential till tapper to look as obvious as possible when they are near a register. Keep displays and merchandise around the register to make it awkward for them to lean over and gain access.

Billing Fraud

Billing fraud is rarely a consideration of the small business owner until after it has happened to them. When the owner himself deals with all check writing, this is not much of a concern, but if the business is large enough to have a support staff, fraudulent billing can be effective.

Means

Those who practice billing fraud consider medium to large companies to be their best target. Companies with a lot of varied inventory or office equipment are perfect victims for this type of fraud.

Methods

Billing fraud may be intentionally fraudulent or simply deceptive. The former is a crime; the latter, unfortunately, is marginally considered creative marketing.

- With intentional fraud, fake businesses send invoices common to the target business. They will avoid billing as a supplier, because they know that most businesses track receiving closely. They usually will bill for administrative costs such as copy machine rental or service. They open a bank account and send out massive numbers of bills to companies, hoping that a portion of them will actually send a check.
- The deceptive advertising manifests itself in nicely tweaked order forms that look like invoices. Some will even have a mock "Okay to Pay" stamp on them, with the appropriate small print to indemnify them from blame. Whatever product they are selling, they hope that the busy office associates will assume that it is an invoice and toss it in the stack of bills to be paid. They do send the ordered product, but it is usually not something you need or want. If it was, they would not have to cheat to get customers.

Proactive Deterrents

- Check and balance systems in invoice processing are important. Make sure that your business pairs all invoices to purchase orders before processing. Some small businesses do not use purchase orders, but it is an inexpensive discipline well worth the time and money.
- Use a unique "Okay to Pay" stamp, not a generic off-the-shelf stamp. Have a line on the stamp for a signature and the expenditure account number that the bill is to be paid from. The unscrupulous business is not going to know what your account numbers are.

Vandalism

Vandalism—or Criminal Mischief, as it is often called—is an annoyance that translates into capital shrinkage. The wanton destruction of property, from graffiti to broken windows and fixtures, is a problem all communities contend with. A business's location is often the only incentive the offender needs to commit this crime. Means and methods are elementary—we all know what graffiti is. Deterrents are few if you are in a neighborhood plagued with the problem, but some steps can be taken.

Proactive Deterrents

- Remote restrooms usually take the biggest hit, and a dirty restroom is a real offense to the customer. Having the restroom near the offices or other high traffic area will help curb that problem.
- As far as outside vandalism goes, the cost of running fluorescent lights is probably the same as the cost for constant graffiti removal but a lot less trouble. Graffiti proof paint will allow the quick removal of graffiti. If the business is targeted relentlessly, the cost of repairs may be less than the cost of a uniformed guard service.

Robbery

Robbery is a delicate matter and one that I do not want to touch on lightly. The disturbing fact of armed robbery is that it is the most unprofitable of crimes yet people still do it. Considering the punishments and the small return, less than $300 in most cases, it is obvious that only really ignorant and violent people commit armed robbery on small businesses. Even the cleverest of bank and vault robbers walk away with minimal cash; those who try to remain long enough to collect more end up with five news helicopters following them up the interstate. Armed robbers will commit crimes in front of cameras, even when there is a monitor right there showing them in full color. Most ten-year-olds will tell you that the clerk cannot open the safe at the local convenience store, but these criminals will insist upon it as if all of television and the media was conspiring to mislead them.

What this means to the security professional is that our only duty with respect to armed robbery is to protect two assets: the employees and the customers. Cash and inventory are meaningless in these situations. We can institute solid proactive deterrents, but some of these idiots will still decide that a six-pack of cheap beer, sixty bucks, and cigarettes are worth risking twenty-to-life in prison.

Means

Robbers perceive a means when they know that cash is present and employees are few. It's no surprise, then, that convenience stores are the top target. The night shift means working alone for most convenience store clerks, and all of their transactions are made with cash. Discount stores are also high targets, mostly because they are usually located in higher-crime neighborhoods. However, even a busy department store can fall prey to an armed robber, so everyone who deals with cash is potentially a victim.

Methods

- *Take-Overs:* Armed take-overs of a business are rare but dangerous. Usually conducted by two or more suspects, employees are forced into submission while the suspects clean out inventory and cash. Organized rings conduct these types of robberies.
- *Old-Fashioned Stick-Ups:* Convenience stores are usually the victims of solo acts—one person with a gun who simply demands money. The danger to employees is high. These types of robberies are compulsive, and the suspect is often under the influence of drugs or alcohol. They are acts of desperation and violence, not money-making ventures. Most shoplifters get away with a higher bounty than stick-up artists.
- *After-Hours Robbery:* Clever robbers will hide in stockrooms or bathrooms waiting for a business to close. Without the nuisance of customers, the robber can take more time directing the associates and collecting his gains.
- *Note Passers:* Many robbers will not even reveal a weapon and just hand a note to the clerk. They may do this even in a busy store while standing in line. They usually target the area of the business where they know change is given to other registers, such as the customer service counters in department stores.

These are some very general categories, and it is important to note that there are many variations. Robbery investigation is a complicated and in-depth subject; we are only interested in reviewing the steps that we can take to preserve life and assist in an investigation. It would be presumptuous and dangerous to assume expertise in this area without extensive training.

Proactive Deterrents

Most of these strategies will not deter the diehard robber, but they will assist in protecting associates and helping police conduct their investigation:

- Closed circuit television and cameras, especially when there is an obvious monitor displaying activity in the store, can dissuade many robbers from striking. At the least, the video evidence is the best support available to a police investigation.

- All associates should be regularly trained on how to conduct themselves in an armed robbery. The key is complete compliance. Give the robber what they want as fast as you can. If you practice this process enough, the associate may even be able to provide vital witness statements after the fact.
- If you have night safes and drop boxes, make sure that there are prominent signs, preferably with graphics for the illiterate, announcing this to customers. Besides acting as a deterrent, it will provide the employee with proof that he or she cannot open the safe. You do not want the robber insisting that the associate can open a locked safe. This kind of confrontation can lead to further violence.
- Stockroom and bathroom checks should be routine measures before closing a business. If you have a central vault, it needs to be remotely monitored by someone during closing, even if it is just an associate in another part of the store.
- Robbers will look for obvious signs of a central register where change and cash advances are obtained. Having a stream of employees carrying money bags to a specific point is like hanging a giant arrow over the main cash location. Either have the associates approach through back areas (monitored, of course) or take change to them. Do not advertise that one specific register is the cash cow of the store.
- If you have security or loss prevention agents and good camera systems, install silent alarms at main registers. The protocol for the loss prevention agents is to observe, record, and communicate to the police. Practice this with some regularity.

Burglary

Burglary is broadly defined in many states. Just entering a business with the intent to deprive qualifies as burglary in some states, such as California. This section is about the traditional concept of burglary: after-hours penetration of a building with the intent to steal cash, equipment, or inventory.

Means

Burglars target businesses that have property or inventory that can easily be converted into cash. A toy store, for instance, probably will never see a burglary unless it was an act of juvenile stupidity. Jewelry, electronics, hardware, and music/video stores would be inviting targets. Businesses with electronic equipment such as recording equipment, televisions, and computers would also be at high risk.

Burglars vary in their preferred target, but basically they look at these factors:

- *Ease of Entry:* How quickly can they get past physical barriers and alarms.
- *Ease of Exit:* How many options do they have for leaving a building.
- *Avenues of Regress:* How close are they to major roads and population centers, and how many routes are available to them.
- *Ease of Conversion:* How quickly can they create cash from the property stolen.
- *Logistics of the Theft:* How easy is the property moved, and how much time will it take to remove and load.
- *Visibility of Target:* Who if anyone will be able to view their activities.
- *Police Response:* In the worse case scenario, how much time will they have before police respond to the location.

Methods

Most criminals will perceive the lack or abundance of means and react accordingly. Burglars are a notch above in that they are masters at creating their own means. They tend to use methods that dictate the opportunity rather than respond to it.

- Burglars are well aware of the slow response time of police to burglar alarms. Many will find a weak door in a building or slide nonconductive metal up into the crack of a door to interrupt the magnetic seals just to set off the alarm. Then they leave, repeating the act several times in a week. The police assume every call is a false alarm. Burglars will watch from a distance and time police response. When they are comfortable, they make their move. I once met a burglar who actually used to go into his target store right before closing and release a rabbit in the far corners. That rabbit would set of every motion detector in the store. After a week of "faulty" alarms, the police would not even respond. The poor security manager lived thirty minutes away, so the burglar had an excellent window of opportunity.
- In assessing ease of entry, some burglars are high-tech and can disable simple alarm systems. Those who cannot make do by hiding until after hours. Then they storm the building, quickly take what has been preselected, and exit to a waiting vehicle out a fire door. No entry problems, no exit problems.
- "Crash and Grabs" have gained in popularity. These burglars work in teams and simply drive a truck into the glass doors of a building, load up and drive away. One department store had a rash of these events in highly trafficked mall stores. After the fifth one it occurred to them to put cement flower pots in front of the exposed doors.

- Businesses with both outside and inside sales areas have to be wary of set-ups. These burglars load carts full of merchandise and push them to outside sales areas. They cover or conceal the carts and leave, returning after closing to snip through the fence and take the prepositioned loot.

Proactive Deterrents

- Well-lit buildings, especially around fire exits, are the least prone to break-ins. If you have skylights, make sure they are lit as well.
- Plan a logical alarm system. When someone triggers a perimeter alarm, they should trigger a motion detector inside as well. If the alarm monitoring service sees an obvious pattern of movement, they can express this to the police.
- If you are at high risk of burglaries, use a private patrol service. Their response time is quick and always faster than the police. They can assess whether or not there is a real situation at hand and communicate with the police.
- Use a quality alarm monitoring service. Make sure their monitoring is comprehensive—some monitoring services separate accounts so that one person is watching perimeter alarms while others monitor internal alarms. One company I worked for had their zones in separate accounts; when an alarm event occurred, I would receive three phone calls from three different attendants who had no idea what the other attendants were reporting. The police did not appreciate three phone calls either.
- Use lighting with motion detectors in high-risk areas of your business. Darkness is a friend to the burglar, and your $100,000 camera system is not infrared. Another company mystery: the business with the poor alarm service required that cameras were turned to record the fine jewelry department after hours. Of course, when a crash-and-grab occurred, they could see nothing on the tape except some bobbing flashlights.
- Again, check perimeter stockrooms, bathrooms, and closets before closing. Your closing personnel should not just run off, but set the alarms and wait a few moments for any indications of problems.
- If you have outside storage or sales areas, keep them clean and require a walk-through at the end of the day to look for out-of-place property.
- Tag your property and equipment, not just with stickers but with indelible marker or etching tools.
- Advertise your deterrents as well as you advertise your product. Stickers and posters warning of marked inventory, alarm monitoring, and private patrols will make the burglar look for a safer target.

- Large warehouses and manufacturers have a bad habit of leaving unlocked padlocks hanging on clasps and chains. Locksmithing is not the most complicated science, and if you have master keys that unlock everything, the good burglar can take a loose padlock home to figure out the key pattern.
- Do not underestimate the need for strict control over alarm pass codes. A clever method is to gain a sales manager's name, find his home number in the phone book, and call him, identifying yourself as the alarm monitoring company. Most monitoring companies request a portion of the alarm code, but not the whole code for identification. But an innocent manager can be coaxed into giving the whole code easily: "Strange, you aren't in the computer. Give me all the numbers on your alarm card . . . Oh, there you are!" Now your entire alarm system has been compromised, and the manager most likely will not even report the incident to you.

4. Elements of Cause: Solid Cases with Minimal Liability

We have thus far assessed our vulnerabilities to external crime and put in place deterrents to dissuade these acts. Still, crime occurs, and as security professionals, we are expected to contain and dispose of these incidents. To do so, we must create an essential part of the loss prevention strategy that outlines the procedures for identifying, detaining, arresting, and processing those who commit criminal acts against the business. For every type of situation that demands a reaction, from shoplifting to vandalism, you will need to have an Incident Response Protocol (IRP) established in writing. This protocol must be as insightful as it is informational. When you, an employee, or another security professional read the IRP, they should derive from that procedural not just solid directions on what to do but a sound understanding of why they are doing it. Without this knowledge, how can the employee make good business decisions when faced with a situation not identical to the IRP scenario?

Pivotal to all aspects of your IRP for external crime is the thorough and earnest appreciation for the liability and risk inherent in arresting suspected criminals. From the moment when you first observe suspicious activity to the moment when the suspect is taken away by the police, there are innumerable opportunities for mistakes and oversights, all of which can invite exposure to lawsuits, criminal prosecution, injury, and sometimes death. A casual regard for this topic can lead to disaster, financially as well as in human terms.

We minimize liability by creating Elements of Cause, a list of conditions that must be present before detaining a person suspected of a crime. These elements are derived from a comprehensive understanding of three subjects:

- *The rights and responsibilities of private citizens when affecting an arrest:* In each jurisdiction, there exists local, state, and federal laws that grant private persons the right to arrest other persons who commit crimes. In addition, there are specific laws in most states that further define the rights of business owners to arrest those who damage or steal their property. The importance of this subject lies in one crucial fact often forgotten by security agents: we are not police officers. As simple and as obvious as that seems, most liability issues stem from overstepping the bounds imposed on private persons both by criminal law and by civil codes.

- *The application of Criminal Law to the business and individual:* Without a clear understanding or what the criminal justice system defines as "illegal," we certainly cannot arrest for criminal acts. But this understanding must extend beyond simply knowing the penal code to attaining an awareness of how the local criminal justice system translates and adjudicates those codes.

- *The application of Civil Law to the business and individual:* While criminal law generally is straightforward and predictable, civil law is continually in flux. The subjective forum of civil courts allows juries and judges to create new precedents daily and these precedents, more than criminal law, are the greatest consideration when instituting your elements of cause. A wrongful arrest will more likely land you in civil court fighting a million dollar tort than land you in jail for false imprisonment. And, while criminal court requires decisions "beyond a reasonable doubt," civil court only requires a majority decision to pass judgment against you. In the same vein, the defendant carries the burden of proof in civil court instead of the plaintiff. There is no "innocent before proven guilty" in civil law as in criminal law. You basically begin the proceeding as guilty and then the jury decides to what degree of guilty you are. Finally, civil jurors do not have to be bound by current law. So even if your state's laws protect the merchant from lawsuits when acting in good faith, the jury is not obliged to consider that law. It's mind boggling when we hear stories of burglars who trip and injure themselves during a home invasion and win judgments against the homeowner, but it is the reality of the civil court system. Thus, our efforts in dealing with external crime must be constrained to avoid the menacing lawsuit.

Rights of Arrests

Most states have included legislation either in the penal code or business and professions code allowing merchants or the agents of those merchants to detain an individual when they reasonably believe that their property has been taken unlawfully. Each jurisdiction varies, and your local district attorney's office will be happy to provide you with the specifics. Five standards, however, are common in each state as far as the right to detain and arrest:

1. The merchant or his agent must have *probable cause* to believe that the suspect is attempting to deprive the establishment of property unlawfully.
2. The detention must be made *promptly and without delay*.
3. The detention is made for the *purpose of investigation*, not punishment.
4. The detention is for a *reasonable period of time*.
5. If an arrest is effected, *delivery to an officer* of the law is made without undue delay.

Cause versus Probable Cause

One of the most misused phrases in security and loss prevention is "probable cause," a legitimate aphorism of criminal law that applies poorly to this field. The civilian application of the rights of arrest is, by the book, nearly as broad as those of a police officer. The only technical difference is that police officers can arrest for a misdemeanor not committed in their presence, while we must directly witness the act. But it is the merger of civil and criminal law that must dictate our use of arrest powers, and this demands stringent policy and procedure.

Because perceptions are difficult to judge, probable cause to you may seem like a weak case to me. Additionally, by law there is no burden for a citizen to understand criminal law as thoroughly as a police officer. Yet, distinctions are made that would only affect those who knew the law. For instance, in most states, you must directly observe the commission or attempted commission of a misdemeanor or infraction. A misdemeanor is a lesser crime, usually punishable only up to one year in prison. An infraction is not a criminal offense, but violation of law resulting usually in fines. Some states, for example, may consider a theft under $50 to be an infraction. However, you may, as a citizen in most states, arrest another citizen for a felony if you have observed that felony or only have reasonable belief that a felony occurred. Misdemeanors require direct observation; felonies can require only a conclusion based on probable cause. Do you know how much someone must steal in your state to commit a felony? Probably not, so criminal law simply is too involved for the average person to grasp.

The defense for John Doe on the street who makes a citizen's arrest of the man who just stole his wallet is that, commonly, theft of a wallet is known to be against the law. Doe does not have to know what the penal code is or whether it's a felony or a misdemeanor. Doe will probably never make an arrest again in his life. Most citizen's arrests are made after the police have made contact with a suspect anyway. This is a formality required in many states, because police officers cannot arrest a suspect for a misdemeanor committed outside of their presence without someone initiating a complaint. They can, however, accept the arrest of a citizen who witnessed and was the victim of a crime, thus taking the bad guy into custody.

The practical application of the law is a mesh of criminal and civil precedence combined with the idiosyncrasies of any given jurisdiction. In one county, bouncing a $20 check can land you in jail, while in another writing checks for $3,000 on a closed account may not even make it to court. The important thing to remember is that the privilege granted by law will not necessarily protect you from civil liability. You must establish the truth of the case. And even when every empirical standard says a theft has taken place, you still have to be critical. Intent to permanently deprive is required to establish theft or fraud, and in the realm of private law enforcement, only the establishment of a crime, not the belief that a crime occurred, will eliminate liability. Therefore, we dismiss this standard of criminal law in favor of a higher standard: arrest for cause, concrete and certain.

Probable cause is defined as reasonable grounds for belief that an accused person may be subject to arrest or the issuance of a warrant. Police officers and the court can operate on the basis of probable cause because the justice system recognizes that due process will offset an error in judgment on the part of the officer or court. Civil law has to extend protection to police officers who make probable cause assessments in good faith, otherwise the criminal justice system would be derailed. Private citizens are not afforded this blanket immunity in civil court. To the contrary, we are actually held accountable to a higher standard, even though the laws in most states extend an affirmative defense to business owners and their agents who reasonably believe a crime against their business has been established. The irony is that "reasonable belief" is a lesser standard than probable cause, but case precedence proves that we cannot afford mistakes in our application of the law. We will be sued and we will lose the majority of time, even when our belief was reasonable or probable. You must understand that civil law is subjective and that even though we can cite defenses established in criminal law, the civil jury cannot be compelled to abide by that defense. They only have to perceive that our actions resulted in harm to the plaintiff; our intentions and justifications are usually not an issue.

For this reason, we should not consider probable cause as the precursor to arrest, but "cause," defined as a ground for legal action. That means a concrete, solid reason for effecting a detention or arrest for external crimes.

For each of the external crimes mentioned in the previous chapter, we will review the elements of cause, the specific requirements that you need to take action. These are the standards that your investigators, loss prevention agents, and guards should live by. They are not conjecture but proved parameters for minimizing liability.

First, let's examine how and why the business can be exposed to liability in arrest proceedings.

The Liability of Arrest

Having seen in the last two chapters the true form of shrinkage and its harsh impact on your bottom line, you or your employees may be straining at the bit to catch a few crooks and show them that you are not a victim but an empowered owner of your domain. These are worthy aspirations; however, they must be balanced with a measure of sobriety when you consider the implications of making arrests. I have participated firsthand in the terrible and gut-wrenching process of explaining to a family the meaningless death of a son and brother over a $100 shoplifting case gone bad. I cannot emphasize enough that there is simply no profit to be made that can counteract the loss of life of you, an employee, or even a shoplifter.

You and those who trust you as an employer are the greatest assets due your protection, and this must be foremost in your mind at all times. The law enforcement aspects of asset protection are an incidental tool, not our focus. Learning about shoplifters and dishonest associates should motivate you to create a culture that repels such acts and minimizes their success. Good business decisions are the charge of the small business, and regardless of the opinions of our eager employees, we must show temperance and a conscientious restraint.

Shootings and personal injury are only part of the difficulty at hand. The liability associated with an aggressive anti-shoplifting campaign is great. In Florida several years ago, a man was stopped by store employees outside a grocery market for stealing a small item. When the man tried to flee, store employees tackled him and piled on top of the man in an attempt to arrest him. The man died of cardiac arrest. The store lost a wrongful death suit and paid millions to the family. This obviously does not represent a good return on investment. The premium increases on the insurance alone would represent thousands of dollars and the publicity is not the kind from which businesses flourish. Yes, the man broke the law, and the merchant did under the law have the right to arrest and detain him, but their zealousness resulted in a death over a few dollars. One could argue that this ending was the direct result of the suspect's poor choices, but imagine if it was your teenage son pulling a bonehead stunt with his friends. Would you honestly face him and say, "Well, you made the choice to steal, son, so now you're dead. I've warned you about the consequences of crime." Of course you wouldn't. You would be enraged at the mishandling of a simple situation. Theft is a crime deserving punishment, but at the hands of the court system, not your employees.

Several factors surrounding a citizen's arrest must be considered: We will look at common torts against businesses from the perspective of civil and criminal law.

A tort is the commission of an act that infringes on the rights of another, rights that are protected by law. A tort claim is the initial step in a civil proceeding where the plaintiff accuses the defendant of the tort and states his intention to seek damages. A lawsuit stemming from the tort claim can be filed against you, your company, your employees, the building owner, and anyone remotely connected to the case (often a lawsuit is served on people so remotely involved it seems ludicrous, but they still have to defend themselves). You may think that since the small business is incorporated, you are extended an umbrella of protection from personal liability. This often is not true in these types of cases—the limited liability afforded to you in regard to company debt does not protect you in cases of gross misconduct or malicious acts.

The major categories of tort claims most often filed against small business owners are:

- *False Imprisonment:* This is the unlawful restraint of one person's physical liberty by another. Imprisonment can result from either physical or psychological confinement. For psychological confinement, the subject has to demonstrate that they reasonably believed that he or she was not free to go due to a perceived threat of force or show of authority. Physical confinement can be construed from nothing more than blocking an exit with your body or positioning a subject so that they cannot easily leave a room.
- *False Arrest:* Once you have formalized the imprisonment by delivering the subject into the custody of police officers, if the arrest was not grounded, then this is false arrest. Remember that a police officer by law has to accept your arrest; it is his duty to take custody of the subject and file your complaint, not question the veracity of your beliefs or statements. Just because the subject drives off in the back of a police car does not mean that the arrest was proper.
- *Assault and Battery:* Often used in conjunction, the two are actually separate charges. Battery is the physical touching of another person without their consent. Battery is very broad—as long as the intent to touch is established the crime can exist. Patting someone on the back, believe it or not, can be battery if no consent is given and there is no privilege to do so. Consent can be implied, for example, long-term friends do not have to give you permission to pat them on the back, nor could you be charged with battery if

you shook someone's extended hand. Assault is any act that causes another person to have reasonable apprehension that a battery is about to occur without consent or privilege. (Privilege refers to an ongoing status between two individuals: a parent does not need permission to touch their own child, nor would a married couple require each other's permission to touch each other. Consent is obviously not extended to abusive or injuring behavior).

Apprehension is the key word: the victim does not have to be fearful, only apprehensive. Battery can also include indirect touch when it is by way of something close to or on the subject's person. Pulling a purse from a subject's arm for instance could be battery, because the intent was to touch via the force of removing the purse. However, unintentional touching is not battery. Brushing against someone on the street while walking cannot be construed as battery. Battery requires intent, but oddly, in most states assault does not necessarily require the establishment of intent. If a person has reasonable apprehension that a battery is imminent, often the intent of the deliverer does not matter. For instance, if you suddenly jumped angrily at a shoplifter, even if you intended nothing more than a lecture, if that shoplifter felt apprehension and reasonably believed you were about to hit him, he could sue for assault. Battery can also extend to unreasonable searches, since touching is involved. Searches are thoroughly covered in the next section.

- *Libel and Slander:* Both terms are for the same tort, defamation. Defamation in general refers to any false statement about a person that lowers that person's esteem in the eyes of others or causes them, to a measurable extent, to be held in disgrace. Libel is the more permanent form of defamation, through print, pictures, or other physical representations. Slander is the less permanent form, through oral communication and gestures.
- *Malicious Prosecution:* Malice is the intent to injure or harass someone or proceeding with an act with callous disregard for their rights. Malicious prosecution is when you cause an arrest without probable cause and where your intent is to use the legal system to injure or harass that person, or you have demonstrated such a callous disregard for their rights that your intent is irrelevant. Accusing a spouse of child abuse simply out of anger, where criminal proceedings were held and the defendant found not guilty, would be malicious prosecution if the plaintiff demonstrated that the spouse's intent was to injure and defame the accused.

All of these torts, except for libel and slander, are both civil and criminal acts. The criminal courts tend to be more conservative in their interpretation of the law, but the civil courts are very lenient in that interpretation. Remembering the fact that in civil court the burden of proof is on you, the defendant, these are the last situations you want to be in.

Can you avoid all of these torts? Can you actually arrest someone who has committed a crime without finding yourself surrounded by tort claims? Absolutely. Affirmative defenses to any of these accusations are truth and privilege. Your privilege to detain and arrest a shoplifter or other criminal is established by law. The truth is up to you.

Elements of Cause of External Crime Arrests

The issues of civil liability, criminal law, and rights and responsibilities of arrest are what shape our elements of cause. As you consider the elements presented below for each type of external crime, understand that these are universally accepted concepts, a product of all those companies that have suffered through a multitude of lawsuits. There is no need to reinvent the wheel here: the big corporations can afford to be legal guinea pigs, the small business cannot. I can state without reservation that every liability incident that I have seen was a result of deviation from these standards. So you must insist on one hundred percent adherence to these elements if you are to avoid the costly price of litigation.

Shoplift Elements of Cause

The following criteria will always ensure that you have embraced truth so that the privilege will protect you. These will allow you to make a lawful *detention*, but do not assume an arrest is in order yet. The seven elements, when followed in total, will assure that shoplifters are prosecutable and have no civil recourse against you.

1. You must observe the suspect *enter into a department*.
2. You must observe the *selection* of merchandise.
3. You must observe the *concealment or carrying out* of merchandise.
4. You must keep *constant observation* of the suspect.
5. The suspect must have an *opportunity to pay* for the merchandise.
6. The suspect must *exit the store* with the merchandise.
7. You must *identify yourself* as having the authority to detain.

It sounds like a lot, but each element is logical and sound doctrine, especially if you consider what happens when you exclude any of the elements.

Entering the Department

Without entry, you cannot account for items already carried by the subject. For instance, let's say you look over and see a woman at a rack of children's blue jeans. She has one of your store bags in her hand. She takes a pair of jeans off the shelf and puts it in the bag. She leaves and you stop her. You had elements 2 through 6, but not number 1.

The problem? She entered the department with a pair of jeans in the bag that she had purchased the day before. Seeing the long lines, she decided to make her own exchange. She put the jeans she had bought on the shelf and selected a new pair, right when you began observing. She has committed no crime. There was no intent to deprive and the even swap was the same thing she would have done in line. You probably just lost a customer as well as exposed yourself to a civil suit.

Selecting the Merchandise

This is so paramount that I am amazed at how many bad stops are made by trained security agents when they do not have this element. Usually, without this, they never had element 1 either. Imagine watching a man standing in front of a sunglasses display place a pair of sunglasses that he is holding into his pocket. You are already thinking critically so you know that this guy probably just put his own glasses away after comparing them to the ones on display. The only time this is not necessary is in the case of obvious "grab-and-runs." These types of thefts are those in which the suspect rushes in, grabs armloads of merchandise, and rushes out. It is reasonable to assume that a person carrying fifteen pairs of unbagged jeans toward the door rapidly is trying to steal.

Concealment of Merchandise

Except in the case of the suspect who carries the item out, which happens often, you must see where and how the item was concealed. Upon detention, you must know where that item is and limit your search to that area. If the person walks behind a display and the item they had disappears, you are taking a great chance if you assume they have the item. You can assume concealment in situations such as fitting rooms, where you personally observe that the fitting room is empty prior to their entry and observe the number of items taken into the room. When the subject emerges without four of the items and you observe that there are four empty hangers in the fitting room, then you have established the concealment. Large bulky items may allow you to establish concealment without directly observing as well. If you see the subject select a tool box, walk behind a display, and emerge without the tool box, then check the display, determine that the large box is not there, and note that the subject has an obvious bulge in his waistline not noted before, you can reasonably establish concealment.

Constant Observation

Losing a subject in nonconfined spaces is a cue to drop the case all together, especially when small items are involved. Most bad stops involve merchandise valued at less than $20. Most bad stops result in settlements of at least $5,000 dollars. Shoplifters, especially your neighborhood opportunist, get startled easy and often drop, or "dump" as it is commonly called, the merchandise they just concealed. If you lose observation then you cannot reasonably establish that the subject still has your merchandise. In the case of small easily pocketed items, I would insist on 100 percent compliance—if there has been any loss of direct sight, even for a moment behind a display or rack, do not stop the subject. In the case of larger items, relative common sense prevails. Our hardware thief above obviously is not going to easily dump the tool box concealed in his pants. If he did, the box would be quickly identified and found in the blind spot behind the display. The customer with four items under her clothes would have a difficult time removing them on the sales floor.

Opportunity to Pay

This sounds trivial, but many a defendant has tried to argue that they thought the register was outside. This is irrelevant in situations where the merchandise is concealed, but in cases where they walk out with the item or use a shopping bag, you need to demonstrate that the registers are obvious and clearly marked. Beware, though, the occasional person who really did wander into the mall not understanding that it was not all one huge store. Use your discretion; your gut instinct will usually tip you off to their intent.

Exit the Store

By the letter of the law, having concealed the merchandise, the attempt at theft has been committed, and that is an arrestable crime. Somehow, in the last few decades, the application of this law has deteriorated, and now absolute intent can only be established by their exit. This makes sense in some cases; an elderly man who places a pack of batteries in his pocket while looking at cards probably is not planning to steal. Also, the lines between shopping bags and purses are blurred, and if a woman can carry a shopping bag why can't a man carry stuff in his pockets until he gets to the register?

In every case of shoplifting, let them cross the threshold and walk out if you intend on prosecuting. Without it, you have a weak case in most jurisdictions.

Identification

It is a weak but commonly used excuse that the suspect did not know who you were and thus can justify fighting or running. The fact that they have committed a crime should predispose them to assuming that someone approaching them does so as the result of their crime. However, while your theft case will not be compromised, if you are assaulted by the suspect, they could claim that they thought they were being mugged or robbed. Identification requires nothing more than a verbal statement of your position. "I work for the store" is sufficient, or the display of a badge also works. Badges are good because they are a universal symbol of authority and bridge any language or cultural gaps.

Return Fraud as a Shoplifting Incident

Another common form of shoplifting is return fraud, such as "pick-up returns," where the suspect picks up an item inside the store and returns it for cash, merchandise, or credit. This happens often in large stores where cash refunds are part of the customer service policy. Return fraud may also occur when they bring merchandise in from outside the business, but even if you suspect the transaction to be bogus, you cannot take action. You cannot establish that the merchandise was stolen from you or another merchant, so there is no proof of loss. For pick-up returns, the criteria are simple:

- You must observe entry into the department, as with shoplifting. Without this, you risk stopping a shopper who was merely picking up an item to compare to others, or had swapped an item that they entered with because it was missing a tag or another superfluous reason.
- You must observe the selection of the item that will be returned. You have to establish with certainty that the item was not carried into the store.
- You must observe the transaction, ensuring that the specific item was returned for cash, credit, or merchandise. This can get confusing, and often it is worth double-checking the transaction in person afterwards to ensure that you did see the transaction as it appeared.
- You do not have to wait for them to exit. The moment the suspect is compensated for the item, you can approach. While they may continue shoplifting or attempt to convert credit slips into cash, the loss is established and you should act immediately. Waiting to see if they do more usually just results in more paperwork, and the recovery of property is the same if you prevent further acts or allow more theft and then apprehend.

Check Fraud Elements of Cause

As previously noted, many jurisdictions will not deal with closed accounts and nonsufficient funds accounts as arrestable crimes. Most district attorney's offices have bad check units that will demand repayments from passers and ultimately file warrants for noncompliance. In the meantime, nothing can stop you from declining a check or telling a customer that they cannot present checks. If you do want to detain or arrest on check fraud, keep these elements in mind:

- You must establish that the suspect had the intent to permanently deprive the business of property or services. You cannot do this in the case of nonsufficient funds. The customer may have just made a deposit or may be "kiting" a check, which means they anticipate that there will be money in the account when the check eventually clears. Even where criminal law specifically reads that writing checks when there are insufficient funds is illegal, the affirmative defense for the suspect can be incompetence or the assumption of payment. The best approach is to decline the check, never to detain.

- In the case of closed accounts, the suspect can still claim incompetence or error. "I picked up an old checkbook" is a common excuse, and you would have to prove that the suspect knew the account was closed and intended to deprive you of the received goods. You cannot prove intent by comparing their actions to what you consider reasonable actions. Without the pertinent information from the bank, such as notices of account closures to the account holder and balance histories, you will not be able to demonstrate intent just because they wrote the check. Again, declining the check is the best choice.

- Though you may not have a prosecutable case, you may detain for the purposes of recovery someone who passes a check on a closed account or has nonsufficient funds. In larger stores, especially department stores, the customer may have made purchases prior to your reviewing the check. Upon determining that the account is invalid or funds are not available, you may approach, identify yourself, and state the reason the merchandise is being recovered. If they choose to leave without giving you the merchandise, then they have, by their actions, demonstrated the intent to deprive and you now have cause for arrest. You gave them knowledge that the payment was void and they chose to leave with the goods anyway. Because they very well could have made an error, this approach should be friendly and discreet. You have the right to recover the merchandise, but undue embarrassment or prolonged detention can still result in civil liability.

- You may have situations where good checks are presented with fake driver's licenses. This does not automatically indicate fraud. Many illegal immigrants open legitimate accounts but use false identification. They have no intent to deprive you of payment. Using a false state identification is a crime, but since it has no impact on the business' assets you should not concern yourself with it. Retaining the false identification is fine if you intend on turning it over to the police. Most busy stores have a small collection of fake identifications that they use for training and eventually give to the police, who shred them. If you establish that the account is not stolen and is legitimate, do not take the check but keep the identification.

- To detain or arrest for stolen checks, you need to establish these elements:
  - The account holder must tell you the checks are stolen. The bank will generally not tell you this information. You need to contact the account holder directly. Sometimes, the bank will call the account holder and have them call you as a courtesy.
  - The account holder must state that the person passing the checks is not authorized to do so. They cannot be a joint account holder or other person with legitimate access to the checks.
  - The passer need only present the check as payment, but having a signature adds forgery to the crime, so wait until the check is signed. You do not need to wait for the passer to exit to approach them. The crime and intent to deprive is established upon presentation of the stolen instrument.
- In the case of counterfeit checks, you must be able to establish that, by virtue of your training and expertise, you can identify the check as a counterfeit instrument. You must also establish that the account number on the check is not valid or does not belong to the name on the counterfeit check, or the person passing the check. Remember the napkin scenario: identifying a counterfeit is not enough; you must show that the reason for the counterfeiting was to permanently deprive, and that can only be demonstrated by showing that the account information was fraudulent.

Credit Fraud Elements of Cause

Credit Card fraud is composed of several crimes:

- *Forgery:* Forgery occurs when a person signs the name of another person on a financial or legal instrument. The person whose name is being forged must be real: it is not forgery to sign an imaginary name. Signing counterfeit checks, where the name on the checks was completely made up and the account number did not exist, would not constitute forgery. With credit cards, though, even if the name of the card is fake, the assumption is that the account number is the financial instrument, and any signature implies authorization of the card holder. So forgery almost always applies.
- *Fraudulent Use of a Credit Card:* Anytime a card or account number is used fraudulently and without permission of the card holder,

this crime applies, even if the card itself is counterfeit. Again, it is the account number that is of value, not the plastic card.

- *Possession or Use of a Counterfeit Instrument:* The nomenclature is different from state to state, but basically it is a separate crime to possess or present a counterfeit instrument. For this reason, even if the transaction is not completed, a crime as been committed merely by presenting a counterfeit card as payment.
- *Theft:* The amount of the fraudulent purchase of services or goods also can lead to basic theft charges.

The elements of cause for arrest vary, and caution should always be applied:

- For stolen cards, the authorized card holder must state that the person using the card does not have permission to use the card. It is not enough to have the bank state that it is stolen—many times someone will misplace their card, report it as stolen, then find it later, forgetting to call the bank. You need to speak to the card holder directly. You need to describe specifically the person trying to use the card. It could be a relative or other person whom the card holder ultimately would not want prosecuted.
- After detention, you need to confirm after identifying the suspect that the card holder does not authorize this person to use the card. If you cannot talk to the card holder, then you do not have a case!
- For counterfeits, cause is established immediately when you, through training and expertise, identify that the card is a counterfeit. You do not need further investigation at this point to make a detention. As long as you are sure that the card is counterfeit, you may detain. You can establish this because you physically examined the card, you established that the account number does not match the embossed numbers, or that the name on the card does not match the bank's records.
- After detention, you will need to contact the bank and the account holder, gaining the same information as above. The police will also directly contact these witnesses.

In most cases, the business will not actually be the legal victim of a credit card fraud. The state recognizes the account holder and the bank as the victims, because the business would have been paid regardless. A charge-back to the company is a civil recovery, so we are still not technically the victims. This fact should dictate your planning incident response to credit fraud. If the business's assets are not threatened, then where is the return on investment in conducting an arrest and a time-consuming investigation?

Of course, if the business issues its own version of a credit card, such as department store cards, then you are the victim and engagement of credit card fraud is essential.

One last point concerning business-issued credit: false applications for credit are only borderline illegal. Just because someone uses a false social security number or identification does not mean that they do not intend to pay their bills. Again, some illegal immigrants will obtain false social security numbers and identification in order to work, get utilities and phone services, and obtain credit. The vast majority have every intention of paying their bills. They are just doing what they feel they need to do to have the basic quality of life most of us take for granted. The violation itself does not establish intent, nor does it impact your profit, so politely reject the application and take no further action.

Counterfeit Currency Elements of Cause

Most of us have unwittingly passed a counterfeit bill at some point. Many remain in circulation for years before being ferreted out at banks. Observing someone pass a counterfeit is not cause for detention. They need to establish a pattern that proves intent. You need to observe a systematic attempt at converting the counterfeits into real money, such as going to different registers throughout a large store making small purchases, or making multiple purchases using counterfeit bills each time. Be aware, though, that even though the presenter of any financial instrument assumes the responsibility of ensuring its authenticity, the law allows for a lack of expertise. Many foreigners are issued counterfeit bills by criminal currency exchange businesses, especially in Mexico and Central America. So even an individual with several bad bills may have been a victim. For this reason, I would be courteous when detaining in these cases. Unless there are aggravating circumstances, such as more than five counterfeit bills or a number of associated people passing bills, do not aggressively approach them. Explain the situation and let them know that they are not in trouble. The customer may very well be out several hundred dollars because of someone else's dishonesty, so don't compound their misery by making them feel like criminals. In most cases, contact the police, not for the purposes of arrest, but so that an outside agency can concur that the bills are counterfeit and take custody of the money. You would not want someone accusing you of taking their money unlawfully. Also, the police report the incident to the United States Secret Service so that the federal government can track and combat outlets for counterfeit currency. If you sympathize with the customer, they will gladly wait to talk to the police and provide them the needed information. Even in the case where the preponderance of evidence points toward criminal intent, let the police make that final determination. You have already saved your business from a loss; don't compromise that success by making potentially false accusations.

Traveler's Checks and Money Orders Elements of Cause

The criteria for detention here is basically the same as for checks and credit cards. If they were reported stolen, you need to talk to the original check holder. In cases of counterfeits, if you can identify them as such, then you can detain the passer. Money orders are generally bearer instruments, which means that whoever has them can use them, so you should avoid dealing with them altogether.

Till Tapping Elements of Cause

There are only two distinct requirements for arresting a till tapper. They must complete the act and you must observe the act. You can immediately arrest when the money is physically moved from the till into their possession, so even if they just have it in their hands you may detain them.

Billing Fraud Elements of Cause

You will probably never actually have an opportunity to arrest someone for this crime because the crime is not complete until payment is received and cashed. This case needs to be referred directly to the police.

Vandalism Elements of Cause

In vandalism cases, it is very important to directly observe the act. It is also important to recognize the affiliation of graffiti with gang activity. Police intervention is the best tactic.

Remember that accidents are accidents, and even if they occur because of neglect or misbehavior, the destruction of property in these matters is a civil issue not criminal. Vandalism must demonstrate an intentional destruction of property. Even if the destruction is secondary to another crime, such as a shoplifter knocking down a display while attempting to escape, the act itself is not criminal.

Robbery Elements of Cause

Your role and the role of your associates in robbery cases will be as witnesses. The elements of cause and subsequent arrests are in the venue of the police.

Burglary Elements of Cause

When referring to the traditional burglary, the act of illegal entry is the only cause you need to call the police. You will rarely have an occasion to directly observe such acts, and if you did, the arrest should be conducted by the police.

Accomplices

The final aspect to establishing cause is knowing when you can also detain someone who appears to be an accomplice. Many lawsuits are won by supposed accomplices who have been arrested incidental to another's crime. Accomplice cases are tricky—they often result in civil liability even when the core case was legitimate. Empirical observation is necessary to establish that a person or persons are actively working in collusion with another to commit a crime. Merely "watching out" or hanging around the shoplifter does not constitute an offense, even if you know that they were obviously involved. It is tempting to detain anyone you might think is participating, but without the elements of cause, you are flirting with the diabolical tort.

You should instruct everyone to adhere to the following guidelines when determining whether a person is an accomplice.

First, the individual must actively engage in at least one of these three elements of the theft:

1. *Selection*, when the act of selection is conducive to theft.
2. *Concealment* of the merchandise.
3. *Carrying out* of the merchandise.

In addition, the individuals must be in *constant contact* with each other.

Having the selection conducive to theft means that while selecting, the accomplice does something to further the act, such as remove tags or hangers, or ball up the merchandise. If this is merely selection, for example, a person hands the thief a shirt and the thief conceals it, you cannot really prove that the first person knew or intended for the thief to conceal it. You must be very careful if this is the only element the person is involved in.

If the person assists in the concealment in anyway, you have a good accomplice case as long as the act is active. They must touch and manipulate the merchandise in this process. Merely being a look-out, even though that helps the thief conceal, does not count. But putting the merchandise in the bag held by the thief does count, for example, as does holding the bag for the thief.

If the person carries out the merchandise and you can demonstrate that they had knowledge that the instrument they were carrying contained stolen goods, then you have a case. If the thief loaded a backpack and then went over and handed the pack to another, and then that person walked out with it, you could not arrest that person unless he or she had witnessed the thief place the items in the pack. You could certainly stop the person and recover the merchandise, but you could not detain him or her. Conversely, if the thief lets that person walk out but remained in the store, you could not amply demonstrate that the thief knew or instructed the other person to walk out. You could not arrest either of them. However, if both walked out together, the second person carrying the pack, you could stop and detain the thief and recover your merchandise from the second person.

If each person is in constant contact with the other, then this is not an issue. By this I mean that all involved suspects have to be witnessing the acts of the others. If one left for the bathroom for ten minutes, they could reasonably argue that they expected the other to pay for the merchandise while they were absent. If they are together, this argument will not work.

Aggregate/Individual

As far as the arrest goes, deciding who is responsible for which merchandise depends on the level of collusion, or cooperation, involved. If two people entered and you observed the six elements for each of them, then they would basically be two separate cases, each held accountable to the items they stole. Just because they stole items at the same time does not make them accomplices. However, if it is an accomplice case as described above, where the fruits of the crime are shared, both participants would be charged for the entire amount, regardless of who selected what. The basic rule of thumb is that if they needed each other to steal, then they are responsible for the totality of the theft. If they stole individually, and the only support was egging each other on, then they are responsible for their part of the theft.

5. Detaining and Processing the External Case

Having understood the liability and law issues presented in Chapter 4, and having established a cause for arrest, you now must take action. The Incident Response Protocol for external theft needs to include a detailed strategy for the following components:

- *Detention:* Taking custody of the suspect.
- *Interview:* The process of gaining required information, including rules of search and seizure.
- *Documentation:* Report writing and evidence handling.
- *Disposition:* The prosecution or release of the suspect depending on objective guidelines that you establish for your company, trespassing the suspect, and issuing a civil demand for restitution.

Detention of Suspects

This is an area of expertise where the highest degree of competency must be demanded of loss prevention personnel. Too many companies underestimate the need for expert tactical training of personnel in effecting an arrest. Arresting someone is not a light matter—you are depriving them of their freedom, and they are well aware that they are facing some form of retribution. External crime suspects may be working with the benefits of adrenaline, drugs, lack of conscience, violent dispositions, or desperation, all characteristics that need to be respected and prepared for.

You must recommend to the small business one of three positions to take when it comes to external apprehensions:

1. *Hands-on Policy:* This is when your loss prevention agents are expected to use reasonable force to take custody of the suspect.
2. *Hands-off Policy:* This is when your agents are expected to approach and not use any physical contact to take custody of the suspect.
3. *Recovery Only:* This is when your agents are expected to effect only a recovery of stolen merchandise, by either "burning" the suspect inside the store, which means using obvious body

language or comments to persuade the suspect to dump concealed merchandise, or by asking for merchandise to be returned without threat of custody or prosecution.

Large companies are caught in a continual pendulum when it comes to deciding which policy they dictate. They oscillate from allowing use of force to allowing zero contact depending on their perceived liability. Most of these policy changes are dramatic, stemming from single instances that provoke an immediate response from high-level executives. The fact is that all of these policies have disadvantages and advantages—it is not the policy that deters or promotes liability, it is the underlying training of agents and the honest assessment of assets that affect the outcome.

Considering the amount of liability carried on the shoulders of our hourly loss prevention agents, it is bewildering how little companies invest in their training. If we expect civilians to conduct arrests on potentially hostile suspects daily, then they need to be trained to do so in a safe and effective manner. All too quickly, agents leave minimal training with a badge and handcuffs and are launched out to battle crime as if these skills are inherent to ordinary people. Police officers spend months learning how to control an arrest situation—most loss prevention agents are lucky to spend hours on the subject.

If your business is not willing to invest in comprehensive training in tactical arrest procedures for their agents, than they need to have a hands-off policy. It is a crime in and of itself to send these young people into a battlefield expecting their triumph at all costs without the armor of training. Even a hands-off approach can result in death if the agents do not understand what they are dealing with. Take this actual incident as an example: two agents attempt to stop a male adult who has stolen about $100 in merchandise. The suspect does not stop walking and continues toward the parking lot. The agents do not make physical contact, instead walking with him trying to coax him into the store. In the parking lot, the suspect suddenly pulls out a pistol from his waist. Agent One reacts by trying to grab the suspect from behind in a bear-hug. Agent Two is in front of the suspect, directly in the line of fire. The suspect fires two rounds into the chest of Agent Two. Agent One falls back in defense and the suspect fires one round into his shoulder, then flees in a waiting vehicle.

Now, did the agents escalate the situation? They did not have physical contact, but they allowed a noncompliant suspect to control the situation. Most larcenists are not going to use a weapon, even if they carry one. But the tension mounts as time goes on, and this suspect is able to gain confidence with every stride. Finally, the suspect draws a weapon. Even then we do not know if his intention was to shoot, but precedent would dictate that he most likely would only threaten.

Agent One sees the suspect move his hand toward his waistband and attempts to take physical control. This unarmed agent may have the suspect's body controlled, but his hands are free to move about. The result is as mentioned.

Analyzing this scenario, we have to critically ask why the agents would allow the suspect to lead them into the parking lot. No police officer would allow a suspect to control the environment of the circumstances. In addition, if the policy was hands-off, then why continue following a noncompliant suspect? What did they hope to accomplish if they were not planning on ultimately using force? If the policy was hands-on, why would they allow the suspect to walk at all? His indication of noncompliance would have authorized their use of reasonable force.

Would the agent have lived if they had used force immediately upon the suspect's exit? There is no way to know for sure, but command presence and tactical positioning certainly could have limited the risk. Would the agent have lived if they had let the suspect walk away? Undoubtedly. Regardless of the other possible outcomes, what is clear is that the agents were not trained in dealing with hands-on or hands-off tactics. The company they worked for failed miserably in preparing them to do their job. In fact, that particular company had absolutely no established training for their loss prevention agents, except for a series of textbook exercises. The training was left up to the unit loss prevention managers, who were likewise not trained in tactics. As a side note, the company's reaction was to institute a hands-off policy in all stores. They completely missed the lesson of this scenario. At minimum, the death of the young agent should have resulted in a serious review of training standards, not an arbitrary change of policy.

Of course, there are many ways to analyze this tragic event, and this analysis is an opinion based on my experiences. The important fact is that a man with a gun and no regard for human life killed an innocent person. As employers, though, we have a moral responsibility not to consider that as an absolving alibi for our own inadequacies in leadership. As a person creating a loss prevention strategy for your company, you have a moral obligation to consider solemnly this and similar incidents when determining a course of action for those employees in your care.

Loss Prevention Assets

The other issue in determining the appropriate strategy for your business is realistically appraising the assets at hand. Here are some points to consider:

- *Personnel:* How many loss prevention or security agents do you have for the business? Can one person maintain control from the camera room while at least two effect the arrest? In high-crime areas, will you be able to have a response of at least three or more officers?

- *Communications:* Do you have an adequate communications system? Are radios affected by blind spots or range? Do agents have to rely on phones and intercoms? Without solid communications, the agents are at great risk.
- *Support:* Are the police quickly available to lend support? Mall businesses may have police substations near by. What kind of support can you expect? Are there other security agencies nearby that would assist or at least stand by? Are any regular employees trained to back up your agents?

Between training and asset development, you can decide a realistic plan for your agents.

Hands-on Policy

If you are going to allow the use of force in making apprehensions, do so only when the training and assets are exceptional. This means practicing scenarios at length with your agents. Your procedures should include all the following:

1. *Liability Training:* Every agent must understand the issues of liability as described in the previous chapter.
2. *Tactical Training:* Agents must learn about approach, command presence, position, and control of the confrontation.
3. *Handcuff Training:* Handcuffs are a great tool for control, but the awkward application of handcuffing can lead to injury and further escalation.
4. *Communications:* Nothing can impede an arrest more than poor radio disciplines. Utilizing an established code eliminates confusion and miscommunication. There must be a uniform reference to exits, locations, and situations.

Tactics in arrest situations are not a training subject to be condensed into a few pages. You need to draw on outside sources to develop a sound training program. My only emphasis here is that if you are going to use force in making apprehensions, commit to the highest quality training possible for you and your employees.

Hands-off Policy

If you realize that the training and assets are not available to safely conduct hands-on arrests, then a hands-off policy can be sufficient. At minimum, the suspect will not return to your store again. Do recognize that thieves have their own community, and it is easy to get a reputation as an easy target. If the word gets out that the crooks can walk away if they are caught, then you can expect an increase in shoplifting incidents.

On the other hand, most shoplifters will comply with verbal commands. We train tactically for the worst-case scenario, not the commonplace occurrence. Even when you allow the use of force, that does not mean that you will always have to use it. The important issue is that if you intend for apprehensions to be nonphysical, then make sure your agents do not imply physical force just to get the suspect back in the store. If the suspect refuses to cooperate, then it should be considered a lost cause.

Recovery-Only Policy

Some businesses choose never to detain but only recover merchandise. This may be a necessity if assets and training are limited. In these situations, uniformed guards are the best deterrent. They can merely look at a shoplifter and the crook will usually dump the merchandise and leave the store. Again, a reputation for leniency may have long-term ramifications and invite more incidents.

Choosing to "burn" suspects does not alleviate the need to follow the elements of cause. The wrong look or comment to an innocent person will at minimum affect the good name of the business, and at maximum result in a lawsuit.

Recovering the Merchandise

Whether you recover the stolen goods outside or inside should be decided case by case. On the one hand, retrieving the items proves undoubtedly that this person did commit the crime. However, if you followed the elements of cause, this should not be a concern. On the other hand, having the suspect reach under his clothes could be tactically dangerous. You have more control inside the store, so often it is worth waiting to recover the items.

Running Suspects

Regardless if you institute a hands-on or hands-off policy, if the suspects are hiding a darker secret or loathe the idea of returning to prison, they will probably run. Wave to them as they go and call the police with an accurate description. Chasing a suspect is dangerous and exposes you to high liability. If someone crashed their car while you darted about the parking lot, you would probably end up paying for it. Even if the suspect was hit by a vehicle while running, you could be liable. Besides, who knows why he is running. He could have a weapon or be on parole for murder for all you know. When the suspect runs, you no longer have control of the confrontation. That is always your signal to step back and let the case go. A good tactical stance will limit the suspect's ability to flee, but some still get through. The small value of recovery in shoplifts does not warrant taking the risks associated with chasing a suspect.

Escorting

Assuming that the crook cooperates, you now get to walk back through the store and into whatever office or space you have set up as a detention area. This is the time to keep the suspect talking. By keeping him engaged in conversation, the suspect cannot think of running or knocking down one of your customers. It also soothes him and you will find that he is a lot more cooperative. Do not play cop or make moral assessments of his actions. You are not there to interrogate the suspect; frankly, if you have all the elements of cause, his statement simply does not matter. The empirical evidence speaks for itself. Just talk. Ask him his name and engage him in light conversation.

Make sure someone walks behind him. Suspects like to drop merchandise if they can while they walk, and the presence of another will also motivate him to behave. Your main concern is safely walking the suspect to the office without interfering with your customers or drawing attention to the suspect.

Associate Response

If you have to rely on regular associates to provide back-up on a stop, pick the ones that you know are calm and have good judgment, and teach them this material. Use a code name for overhead speakers, like "Simon" or "Mr. Jones." When you know that you are going to make a stop, have someone announce "Simon, to cosmetics" or some location that indicates the door you believe the suspect is going to exit. You may use two names, one to indicate urgency, the other to indicate a quiet mobilization. Those assigned to your response team can exit quietly and wait outside. This is not so that you can get into a fight and win; this is because a show of calm force usually de-escalates the situation immediately.

Interviewing the Suspect

The interview consists of all the time you spend with the suspect in custody. Generally, a reasonable detention is considered to be one and a half hours. This means that you must make the attempt to deliver the suspect to a police officer within that time period. Control during an interview is very important. A specific area of the business should be designated as an interview area, free of loose merchandise or fixtures. The suspect should sit in a position without immediate access to you, but where you can always watch while preparing your report. Always make sure that a same-sex witness is present to avoid any claims of abuse.

Some agents seem to have watched too many syndicated television shows about law enforcement and feel compelled to carry out a lengthy interrogation. This is altogether unnecessary except to boost the ego of the occasional overbearing agent. The fact is that your case is solid because you observed the elements of a crime. Their motivation is not an issue. Their intentions for the merchandise or money are not an issue. The police are going to ask all of these questions and whatever references to statements you make in your report will be ignored. A good defense attorney will zoom in on your recollection of statements. They will try to show that you coerced the suspect into admissions or asked misleading questions. It is a can of worms that is unnecessary to open. You have done your job. You have effected a lawful arrest. Let the police worry about the microscopic details.

Search and Seizure

At the beginning of the interview, you need to recover the merchandise from the suspect. Explain to him what you are doing. If the merchandise is in a precarious spot, such as in the suspect's underwear, leave it there and let the police find it. If you intend to let him go, then tell him that he will be free to go and then ask him to give you the merchandise. This will keep him from pulling out a weapon if he has it. Don't be specific about what items you are looking for. You may be surprised at how many things he takes out and places on the table.

You may choose to recover the items yourself. If you are uneasy, it is your right to pat down the suspect for weapons. This is not routine, however. You must be able to verbalize your reasonable concern that prompts the pat down. A nervous suspect can, if you are reasonably concerned, warrant a pat down. Beyond this, however, legally your search is limited to the recovery of the merchandise. If your suspect has a purse, for instance, but you never saw anything concealed in the purse, you have no right to search that purse. You may not empty pockets or search areas unrelated to your observations. If the items are hidden in a stroller, you may search the stroller. You may not search the owner of the stroller, except to check for weapons. You may move purses or briefcases out of the reach of the suspect but not out of sight. If the identification of the suspect is in the purse, then you can ask permission to retrieve it. At anytime, using requests rather than commands is the best option. This covers you in the cases of most tort issues. The request is still cognitively processed by the suspect as a command, sort of like a parent asking a child to hand them something. The child is not going to say no, but the sense of empowerment makes the child willing to participate and act.

Agents who make it a point to go through everything the suspect is carrying are out of line. They are violating the rights of the suspect. The police may conduct a thorough search when they arrive because the suspect is being taken into custody. Our searches must be limited to reflect our observations.

Report Writing and Record Keeping

When you arrest a person, this is not an act to be considered lightly. If you are a police officer, your reports and records are essential. They are no less important as a citizen making an arrest. If you find that you are arresting several people a week, good records are cardinal. I find that on most externals, I can get a court notice after only a week and not remember the case or the suspect's name. As with any administrative tedium, the routine becomes less interesting with time and thus less memorable.

Writing a solid report will keep you out of court. Security agents and business owners who chronically have to appear in court usually write bad reports. To the defense attorney, a lack of written communication skills translates into a lack of verbal skills, and that means a chance for them to win a case. You do not want to be on the receiving end of questions from a defense attorney—they are often very sly and have many tricks for getting you off track. All they need to do is undermine your credibility or confuse the jury and they can win.

Of course, nothing can beat a good videotape, but from time to time you may be arresting purely on your observations. Additionally, police will respond faster and with more enthusiasm when they know that you are organized and thorough. The police can attach your report as evidence and not have to write a redundant lengthy report of their own. They really appreciate the security professional who excels at report writing, and you never know when you could use their help in other areas.

Your case file should be kept for a minimum of three years. I would suggest the contents as follows:

1. Report face sheet
2. Narrative
3. Continuation, if necessary
4. No sales receipts from the register, if applicable
5. Copy of Civil Demand

6. Copy of Trespass (a notice to a person stating that they are no longer allowed to enter or remain upon your property)
7. Photo of suspect
8. Photo of merchandise if required in your jurisdiction
9. Additional supporting evidence (receipts, return slips, etc.)

A simple manila folder can hold all of this, file easily, and be readily accessible for review if needed. Consistency in this organization will ensure that every case is complete and that cases are understandable to all associates, not just the report writer.

Report Face Sheet

This report format is in Appendix C, "Forms and Templates," so that you can copy and use it, or adapt it if you are skilled at desktop publishing. I would suggest use of a typewriter or word processor for filling in the blanks—a lot of people will end up reading your report. The report example in Table 5.1 shows the elements of a good face sheet. These are some guidelines for filling out the report accurately.

1. Fill in the header section before you make copies so that you do not have to write in business information each time.
2. Keep a store case number log sequentially. Also, write in the police report number if it is immediately available.
3. The incident description should be brief and to the point.
4. For the time, use the time that the crime took place. Also, write in the time the suspect is released on their own or to the police.
5. Fill in as much information as you can about their address, employment, and so on. This will assist in your civil demand. If the police find out that the suspect provided false identification, they will amend your report to reflect the true information.
6. For juveniles, contact the parent as soon as possible. It is better to have the parent wait with their child while you complete the report than keep the child in your custody for extended periods.
7. Recovered/salable refers to merchandise that you have recovered that can be resold. Unsalable meant that it was damaged or destroyed specifically due to the suspect's actions. Lost means that you did not recover the merchandise but can account for its value.

Determining Value of Merchandise

Most state laws describe the value of property as the "fair market value." This means that the value would be established by what people would pay for it. Therefore, always list retail as the price, never cost. Even if your price of an item is more than another store's, as long as people choose to pay your price, then it is the fair market value. In the

Table 5.1   Asset Protection Incident Report Face Sheet

ASSET PROTECTION INCIDENT REPORT

Store: ShrinkFree Co.	Unit No.: 0001	Telephone No.: 555-1234

Address: 100 South Anywhere Street, No Place City, CA 90000

Customer	Adult	Prosecuted	Store Case No.:
Associate	Juvenile	Yes No	98-00001 / PD 43563-98

Incident Description   Shoplifting, $140 concealed in purse

Date of Occurrence 04-04-98	Time 13:45 / 14:56	Report By Joe Agent

Last Crook	First Mary	MI J	Alias N/A

Street Address   500 Dependency Way

City Probation City	State CA	ZIP 90000	Telephone No. 555-4321

Soc. Sec. No. 555-00-1234	Place of Birth Somewhere	Race C Sex : Male Female

D.O.B. 03-15-67	Height 5'05"	Weight 145	Hair / Eyes Brn/Blu

Clothing	Place of Employment	Identification Type	Number
red jacket, slacks	None	ID CARD	12345A

Parent/Guardian   N/A   Notified Time   N/A   Release Signature   N/A   Time   N/A

	Quantity	Stock number	Description	Price Each	Total
E	1	1234X	Cologne, Stinky	$40	$40
V	1	5432X	Shirt, blue	$50	$50
I	1	5433X	Dress, silver	$44	$44
D	3	6789W	Hairpins	$ 4	$16
E					
N					
C					
E					

Grand Total: $140

Recovered/Salable $140	Recovered/Unsalable $	Lost $

Photos Taken	Evidence Held	Civil Demand	Trespass
Yes No	Released to Police	Yes No	Yes No

case of sale prices, you as the merchant are taking a loss in theory to boost sales. The sale price is below fair market value, so list the regular retail price, not the sale price. However, in the case of clearance items or items marked-down because of damage, you have made a price adjustment because you could not sell it for the original retail price. So you would list the clearance price, because that is the fair market value.

Narrative

Writing a shoplifting narrative is very simple. People tend to get too wordy and to include irrelevant details. The only thing that matters is the seven elements, and your report will follow that list. Chronology is important. Avoid stating things in your report that you actually find out later. For instance, if you are on a black and white camera system, do not state "I observed that she was carrying a red purse." You know that now, but not at that point of the observation. Also, sentences like, "She then concealed the items in a shopping bag, which she had carried into the store" are awkward and leave room for questions like "How do you know she carried the bag into the store? Could she have picked it up off the floor?" This can be very important, especially in those states where intent prior to entry makes the theft a burglary.

Box 5.1 is a simple shoplift report. Most never need to be more than a page in length. Complicated cases, such as credit card cases, require a lot more detail, but the simple rules apply.

Remember your elements for cause?

1. Entry into department.
2. Selection of merchandise.
3. Concealment of merchandise.
4. Constant surveillance.
5. Opportunity to pay.
6. Exit of the store.
7. Identifying authority.

Notice that the superscript numbers throughout the report identify each of these elements wherever they appear.

There are a few key elements and points that you should emphasize when writing a report:

- In the first paragraph, you establish the time and date, your authority, and the means of observation. You then state the initial contact, your first observation of action. In this case, you have the benefit of seeing her enter, which means that you have element 1 completely.
- Writing numbers as "one (1)" avoids confusion when multiple copies are made and numbers become blurred.

Narrative   Case No. 98 0004   Page __1__ of __1__   No. of Suspects __1__

On this date at approximately 5:45 P.M., I, Joe Manager, employed as a loss prevention manager for Happystore, U.S.A., was observing the sales floor via CCTV. I observed one (1) female adult, later identified as FINGERS, Iva R., hereafter referred to as Fingers, enter the store[1] via the north entrance. I observed that Fingers was carrying a large purse over her right shoulder. I observed Fingers approach[2] a display of cologne and remove from the display one (1) bottle of cologne. Fingers then walked behind a display on the perimeter wall and placed the cologne in her purse,[3] so that it was concealed from sight. Fingers proceeded to the Women's department[1] where she selected[2] one (1) shirt from a display. Fingers removed the hanger from the shirt and then removed the store tags, dropping the tags on the floor. Fingers then placed the shirt in her purse.[3] I observed Fingers select[1] from a rack one (1) dress and one (1) sweater. Fingers placed the dress inside the sweater so that the dress was not visible. Fingers proceeded to the fitting room where she entered. Approximately five (5) minutes later, Fingers exited the fitting room. I observed that she was carrying the sweater but I could not see the dress. Fingers placed the sweater on a table. At my direction, an employee, George Smiles, checked the sweater and reported to me that it did not contain the dress. Smiles also checked the fitting room and reported to me that neither the dress nor any other merchandise was in the fitting room.[4]

I observed Fingers approach[1] the exit. Fingers selected[2] from a table display three (3) hairpins and placed them immediately in her purse.[3] Fingers then exited[5] the store, passing four (4) open registers[6] and making no attempt to pay for the merchandise concealed in her purse.

I stopped Fingers outside, identifying myself with badge and verbally as the loss prevention manager.[7] Fingers was escorted to the office without incident.

During the interview, Fingers removed the described cologne, shirt, dress, and hairpins from her purse at my request.

Fingers made no statements.

Fingers had no money on her person. The purse was empty other than the merchandise.

Fingers was trespassed from the store for two (2) years and referred into the custody of Happyville Police.

Report By: Joe Agent Date: 04/13/98 Signed: Joe Agent

Box 5.1   Asset Protection Incident Report Narrative/Continuation Sheet

- Even though the concealment itself is all you need, comments about behavior that directly facilitate the crime are important. Removing ink tags, price tags, hangers, or balling up merchandise should be mentioned. Don't make assumptions, however: statements such as "She looked around to see if anyone was watching" won't stand up, unless you can prove your psychic abilities. "She looked around from side to side and appeared to be nervous" would be a fair statement.
- In this case, you lost constant surveillance when she entered the fitting room. You have to worry about the dress and the items already

concealed. Since she has entered a confined area, you can document that you checked the area (and in this case the sweater, to make sure some or all of the merchandise was not inside) to logically deduce that she still had custody of the merchandise. Constant surveillance is more about control then direct observation.

- Remember to note that you identified yourself, especially if the suspect attacked you.
- Statements by the suspect are not that important—they do not really have credence in court and, more importantly, your physical case should be beyond challenge. However, if the suspect comes up with a really far out excuse, you can report that, and then report why the reason given was not possible. The real statements will be made to the police, so do not feel a need to interrogate the suspect. Casual conversation is best.
- If you find extra merchandise that you identify as your own, but did not see it concealed, you can keep it and add it to the crime. You may catch the shoplifter in the latter part of the act, and discover more merchandise then you thought. Just add, "In addition to the aforementioned merchandise, I also recovered from her purse one (1) _____ that I identified as store merchandise. Fingers had no receipt for that property."
- Noting whether she had money or whether a purse or another item looks like it was carried only to shoplift solidifies intent. In some states, this will lead to a felony burglary charge rather than theft, regardless of the dollar amount.

Evidence Handling

Some jurisdictions will require you to hold the actual merchandise until after a conviction. This can cause shrinkage in itself if you do not keep close track of this. In these cases, a simple brown bag with the case number and defendant's name will do. Most jurisdictions only require a photograph. If you can, photograph the suspect and the merchandise together to firmly establish the connection. If the officer retains the pictures, take duplicates for your record. Check the local laws regarding whether or not you can take pictures of juvenile suspects. In some states, it is not allowed.

No Sales

A clever trick for a shoplifter is to have a friend come in after they are arrested and purchase the item that they had stolen. Then the friend gives them the receipt and they present that receipt in court. In cases where there is no video, this can really work. If you have no video, then immediately after a detention have someone ring a "No Sale" on every open register. Attach the No Sale receipts to your report. Now the journal tapes are all marked and you can show the judge that there is no way that the new receipt had anything to do with the theft. Who knows, maybe the DA will prosecute the friend who falsified evidence!

Case Disposition

Your final actions in regards to the suspect are geared around two considerations:

- What can I do to ensure that this person does not cause further loss, and
- What can I do to recoup likely undetected losses as well as the cost of payroll and equipment involved in the case?

You answer those questions by deciding whether you will prosecute or release the suspect, whether you will seek damages through civil restitution, and whether you will use the right of trespass to keep the suspect from returning to your property.

Arrest versus Release

Contrary to popular opinion, few states actually require you to tell a suspect that they are under arrest during or directly after the commission of a crime. This saves you the anxiety of creating tension by blurting this out initially. If you feel the suspect is going to go ballistic the moment he or she realizes that jail is looming in their future, call the police immediately after apprehension. They may be annoyed at sitting idle while you write your statement, but just explain that you did not feel safe.

At some point, the suspect will realize that they are not going home that night. Hopefully, you have established a good rapport by that time and the suspect will take it well. Usually, aside from unending begging, your suspect will just wait for the inevitable.

Deciding whether to refer suspects over to the police or release them is a difficult concern. Releasing all your shoplifters may result in increased shoplifting, which is not the goal of the program. Many shoplifters talk with others about their escapades as freely as you or I would discuss tennis. If a store is perceived as being lenient with shoplifters, it can quickly become a target in tightly knit neighborhoods that suffer from above average crime rates. Often, though, especially in the case of otherwise social individuals, it is an embarrassment they would rather never be revealed. Case by case, you can determine if you think your store will be negatively or positively impacted by their release. In areas where police response is slow, it may be costly to sit and wait for over an hour. You may establish your criteria by dollar amount, quantity of items, or types of items. Whatever your criteria, however, be consistent. An arbitrary approach to arrests can result in discrimination suits by a suspect. Establish a minimum dollar amount for prosecution based on your average item price. In an electronics store, you may choose to prosecute for everything because of the high retail of most items. In a convenience store, prosecuting someone for a pack of cigarettes is a terrible waste of your time. This you must determine on your own.

As a rule, children twelve and under are not considered culpable for their crimes and Mom and Dad will probably be enough intervention. The very elderly often are not aware of their acts and also should be released. Anyone with an obvious mental disability should be released to their guardians. The rest of the spectrum is up to you.

Civil Demands

Written into the penal codes of most states is a Civil Demands law that allows you to recover civil damages whether or not you prosecute. The amount can be the cost of the merchandise, if it is unsalable or not recovered, plus fines of up to $500. You can pursue this yourself by writing demand letters and using small claims court, or you can find a service that does it for you. In the case of juveniles, Mom and Dad get to pay, so you can make some decent income from this. The goal of the law is to help merchants offset the cost of equipment and personnel. Make sure you take advantage of this law.

If you do use the Civil Demand process, give the suspect a copy of a signed Notice of Civil Demand. This is not a demand, just a notice (sort of like a tort) that you are going to collect. There is an example of the civil demand notice in Appendix C, "Forms and Templates."

Trespass

Trespass is a broad term; it literally means "to encroach," among other definitions. In criminal law, as it applies to property, trespassing is the act of interfering with the right of possession of a property owner. Simply put, if someone is on your property without permission, they are trespassing and can be arrested.

In the case of any business that serves the public, however, permission for the public to enter and remain upon that private property is implied. After all, how silly would it be to have to give every customer permission before they stepped into your store. When you trespass an individual, you are withdrawing that permission for the individual to enter your property. As with everything in loss prevention, it is a mix of civil and criminal law that molds our trespass policy.

Most state laws allow you to trespass any person who disrupts the usual flow of business. What qualifies as disruptive is left up to the business owner. Shopping malls, for instance, have lengthy codes of conduct dictating appropriate attire and behavior (i.e., no running, no offensive clothing, no loitering). The mall owners can argue that all of these things disrupt business. Obviously, then, a criminal act fully qualifies as disruptive. The suspect's privilege to enter your property needs to be revoked.

The person being trespassed first has to know what acts constitute a disruption of the business. A reasonable person knows that crime is disruptive, so you don't have to post signs saying, "Thieves, drunkards, and vandals will be trespasssed." However, if your implied consent to the public hinges on their abiding by certain rules outside the scope of criminal law, such as dress codes and rules on soliciting, make sure those rules are well posted. Without this posting, you cannot prove that a decision to kick out a person or persons was based on established policy. Those people can claim discrimination and you have no real defense. So if you hate red baseball caps, that is your prerogative, but be prepared to hang one huge sign stating that no one may enter wearing a red baseball cap. Once a person commits the disruptive act, you must give them notice, either verbally or in writing, that the implied consent granted to the general public has been withdrawn from that individual. That Notice of Trespass, regardless of the legal jargon required, is you saying, "You aren't allowed to come here anymore."

Now that they have been served notice, you must give them a reasonable opportunity to comply. You cannot, for instance, trespass your shoplift suspect who you have in handcuffs and then arrest him five minutes later because he remained on your property. Obviously, he is under arrest and cannot comply. If you tell a person to leave your store and they choose to walk really slow, they are demonstrating compliance, even if they are being insolent about it. If, however, they flat out refuse to leave, then they can be arrested for trespass.

Assuming they do comply, then you now have grounds to arrest the trespassed person if they return in the future. They now have no more permission to enter your business than a burglar has to enter your home.

Consistency in the application of your trespass policy is very important. If your policy states that all shoplifters will be trespassed, then trespass every shoplifter. Subsequently, prosecute every trespassed person who enters your store without permission. If you pick and choose who you trespass or who you arrest for violating that trespass, then you open yourself up to charges of prejudice and discrimination. Regardless of the explicit candor of the criminal law, civil juries won't tolerate instances of perceived discrimination. If you trespass one person of one race and don't trespass one of another who commits a similar crime, then you are left wide open for a civil suit, even if it was an innocent omission. If you do not have the resources to consistently apply a trespass policy, you are better off not having one at all. Many large retailers no longer issue trespass notices specifically because their security agents applied the policy inconsistently.

If you do choose to trespass, use a form similar to the Notice of Trespass included in Appendix C. While a verbal trespass is technically enough, having the signature of the trespassed person takes away all doubt. If that person refuses to sign the trespass, indicate their refusal on the form and have a witness sign that you verbally trespassed the subject.

One last but important note on trespassing laws. You do not have the right to detain someone for no other purpose than to trespass them from your property. You can only detain someone when a criminal act has been committed. So if you want someone to leave because of dress code violations, soliciting, loitering, sleeping, singing too loud, or wearing red baseball caps, you cannot take them to your office first, demand identification, or tell them to stand up against the wall while you take their picture. It is false imprisonment. Shopping malls and amusement parks do this all the time, and if those patrons know the law, those establishments would be neck deep in litigation. Every time you see a mall security guard forcing a group of kids to stand in place while someone runs and gets the camera, you are watching a violation of both civil and criminal law. When a customer violates a non-criminal code that you established, you can tell them that they need to leave. You can't tell them that they have to stay or force them to give you identification just because they violated some little rule you created.

It is very easy to become caught up in the excitement of catching criminals. After all, who does not enjoy sending the malfeasant to prison and cleaning up the streets of America. However, you must cling to this singular thought during every interaction with a criminal: Is this a good business decision? Am I protecting an asset of the business I represent?

Remember, your intention is not to minimize crime but to minimize shrinkage. Whatever avenue you choose to take, keep the bottom line in mind.

6. Internal Losses: Associate Dishonesty

Nothing is more demoralizing for the business owner than discovering associate defalcation. You have given someone a job and a good working environment, and yet they abuse your trust. Associate theft usually has a greater impact then shoplifting, not in numbers but in cost. Dishonest associates will steal thousands of dollars if they find a method that goes undetected. There is no great mystery to catching employee theft. These investigations are about methodology not stunning insight. An experienced investigator may detect and resolve problems faster but the techniques are still the same.

Three conditions are required for an associate to commit dishonest acts, just as in external cases:

1. Motivation,
2. Means, and
3. Method.

If you are aware of the essence of each of these, you can deter most employee theft and detect the remainder.

Motivation

Dishonest associates steal for many of the same reasons shoplifters do. They may simply want things that they cannot afford. They may have debt or living expenses beyond their means. They may steal from companies for a living and consider their paycheck incidental to a higher goal. The motivations of Wanting, Needing, and Using apply here as well as to external theft.

Many otherwise honest associates will steal when faced with an overwhelming need, like a surprise pregnancy, financial problems, or divorce. Being aware of your associates' personal life can be accomplished through daily observation, from noticing the car they drive to the shoes they wear. Sudden changes can predict turmoil and future problems. The new employee may replace his station wagon with a sports car, only to discover that the impact of this expense is greater than he anticipated. Moodiness, excessive tardiness, or fatigue can indicate problems at home. These conditions can drive associates to making poor decisions.

Some associates may be angry at the company and feel a need to enact revenge via theft. The store culture can have a powerful effect on the actions of employees.

Motivation for employee dishonesty may not always appear obvious. A bad attitude is easy to detect, but many who steal exclusively for greed are very calculated in their approach. They may work extra hard to establish a positive image in your eyes. They may be quick to catch shoplifters and very friendly with management. I often found that associates who were excessively friendly toward me soon became thick case files on my desk.

Obviously, many are just eager to please, and you do not want to deflate their morale by being distant and cold. Just do not ignore those in your peripheral vision as you look forward at those who keep their distance. When it comes to shrinkage, be as objective with your best employees as you are with your worst.

Human Resource Issues in Loss Prevention

Personnel issues can significantly impact the frequency and size of associate defalcation cases. Your human resource strategies can strongly influence whether an associate is motivated to support the business' mission or work against it through dishonest acts. Wages, awards, retention, tenure, and management style can greatly affect the employees' state of mind as well as their willingness to support store programs and your goals. The University of Florida 1997 National Retail Security Survey solicited human resource information from businesses, including questions on associate compensation, part-time versus full-time staffing, managerial turnover, and associate turnover. The respondents also provided their shrinkage percentage of net sales. Using that percentage as a comparative gauge, the survey results revealed relatively consistent correlation between the levels of compensation, turnover, etc., and the business' shrinkage levels. Of course, like any survey, it is not scientific, and we could argue that the survey results could not specifically isolate the effects of external losses versus internal losses. And we have already discussed in Chapter Two how arbitrary it is to compare businesses with the shrinkage percentage to net sales figure. However, the university researchers did strive to solicit responses from a relatively analogous sampling of retailers, and the resulting pattern certainly is commensurate with common sense.

Overall, the survey results support good human resource doctrine that are by no means surprising, but often ignored for the sake of immediate profit. As you consider the following breakdown of the survey categories, think also how the same factors would affect your customer service, sales, and productivity. Shrinkage prefers the company of other ailments. Like a fever, it is often the harbinger of more abstruse maladies.

Compensation

Generally, those businesses who compensate employees at 10 to 15 percent above the median enjoy lower shrinkages then those who are 10 to 15 percent lower than the median wage. Associates are less likely to compromise a higher-paid position, and they tend to have higher loyalty toward the company. Associates who perceive themselves as underpaid are prime candidates for dishonesty. Within the +/- range of 5 percent, the numbers are inconsistent, usually because large department stores pay around 5 percent above median and experience higher shrinkage levels then smaller specialty businesses.

Analyzing the trend, you may be able to safely assume that an investment of paying 10 percent or 15 percent above median may save you money in the long run. This would be difficult to quantify until you were in business for a few years and could see a pattern of shrinkage results. One thing is certain: employees work harder and have greater loyalty when they know that they are being well compensated. You can draw from a better hiring pool and have better retention. A tight approach to wage levels may look good on the monthly P&L, but it can adversely affect your bottom line.

Part-Time Employees

From personal observation, I can fully agree with the survey finding that part-time employees are more prone to steal then full-time employees. This is especially true of seasonal hires who know that they are leaving and have little motivation to do anything except the minimum required to receive a paycheck. Full-time associates with benefits view their work as an important aspect of their lives and have higher loyalty and a sense of ownership.

The survey reveals that those companies that are staffed 81 to 100 percent with part-time employees experience over a 33 percent higher shrinkage rate then those who hired 71 to 80 percent part-timers. The 81 to 100 percent stores also had shrinkage levels nearly three times higher than those stores with less than 10 percent part-timers. This can translate into a lot of cash, more than you would probably spend on benefits packages. Again, your own financial analysis would determine whether investing in full-time associates is more cost-effective than the resultant shrinkage of hiring part-time employees. It is a very cogent hypothesis that shrinkage will increase or decrease proportionately with the percentage of part-time employees.

Managerial Turnover

Consistent leadership can drive down shrink. High managerial turnover is indicative of mediocre managers who tolerate poor performance and do not enforce the disciplines established. Stores with less than 10 percent managerial turnover tended to experience approximately 30 percent less shrinkage then those with 31 percent to 100 percent turnover. Developing an excellent managerial and supervisory team is the only way to ensure that your asset protection strategy has the anticipated effect.

Associate Turnover

The same criterion holds true for this category. Associate turnover directly reflects on the other categories in that high turnover usually stems from low wages and benefits as well as morale issues stemming from poor management. The survey demonstrated that those stores experiencing less than 10 percent associate turnover had a shrinkage level nearly 40 percent lower than those respondents with 91 to 100 percent turnover. The incremental levels in between were relatively proportionate to these extremes.

This is an essential lesson for the business owner. It is very easy for them to view each element of their business myopically, focusing in on the immediate impact without considering the long-term effects. As you accumulate data while your business grows, each business decision must be viewed with this in mind. You may find that an important part of your success in loss prevention depends on mastering human resource issues.

Proactive Deterrents in Human Resources

Before we discuss the specific means and methods of employee defalcation, here are some essential proactive strategies that you should encourage in the human resource arena that can eliminate motivation toward criminal acts.

Hiring Processes

You can easily eliminate employee candidates who are motivated to steal by weeding them out of the hiring process. Some associates are so intent on theft that just gaining access to a store is the only motivation they need to conduct fraudulent acts.

Past Employment Verification

While most employers will only tell you the dates of hire and last position because of strict human resource laws, you can usually tell from the tone of their voice whether the interviewee was a viable or poor employee. Also, employees who were fired often fudge the dates to make it look like they resigned to join your team, when in actuality they have been searching for a job for months.

Criminal Conviction Checks

Services exist that can check public records quickly and cheaply for you. Most applicants lie when asked about criminal history. If they tell the truth, don't necessarily dismiss them as a good candidate. People do make mistakes and some can change. Having the moral courage to tell you up-front that they have a criminal record can be a good sign, depending on the crime and your business. You cannot necessarily fire someone for having a conviction, but you can fire them for lying on their application if you discover the conviction post-hire. You certainly cannot be compelled to hire anyone that you do not want, equal opportunity standards notwithstanding.

Drug Screening

Drug use is an expensive habit and many employers have turned to pre-employment drug screening to ferret out users. As well as being a defalcation risk, many states consider drug addiction to be a disability once you have hired them, which means you have to pay for rehabilitation or short-term disability benefits. A drug-using associate can also turn the most menial of tasks into a safety hazard.

Reference Checks

Amazingly, few employers actually call the references. The quality of the references can mean a lot. If a young person has the recommendation of a professional who has observed their work firsthand, this certainly means more than a recommendation from a casual friend. Also, charitable activities, extracurricular activities, and involvement in social organizations are indicative of a healthy well-integrated person.

Worker's Compensation Review

Some states treat worker's compensation claims as public record, and companies can access those records and give you a risk assessment. Relative to the number of years worked, one or two claims really does not indicate a problem, but if a pattern of abuse or incompetence is uncovered, these employees can cost you a lot. You cannot fire anyone because of a Worker's Comp claim, so once you hire them, you may be stuck with an expensive liability. Don't be surprised if your state has privacy provisions protecting claimants—this is the inclination in most jurisdictions.

Education Verification

Many interviewers do not even bother checking education levels. If that education is directly tied to the job expectations, you could be placing yourself at risk of liability. For instance, if your store policies required a high school diploma for all security agents, as a minimum level of competency, and then one of your agents wrongfully arrested a customer, it would not be helpful if the plaintiff's attorney discovered that the agent never passed ninth grade.

Credit History Checks

A pattern of delinquencies and charge-offs over a period of time can indicate that a person is irresponsible and even criminal in their financial life. Credit problems in short periods usually just show a one-time problem, like loss of a job or high medical bills. For anyone handling cash, a credit check is a good tool, though it is more costly than other screening programs. You cannot deny employment solely on the results of a credit check, but then again, you do not have to explain why you do not hire people anyway, so wait for a better candidate.

Multiple Interviews

This is a great tool for unearthing the potential dishonest employee. The trick is for the first interviewer to write down the applicant's responses to a list of questions. A few days later, invite the applicant back for a second interview with another manager/supervisor. Have the same questions asked, but slightly reworded, and record the answers. Chronic thieves are chronic liars, and their attempt at deception will be obvious.

Bonding

For high-value, high-cash positions, bonding or insuring the associate can be a good plan. The best benefit is that the insurer will do almost all the above to make sure they are not taking a risk.

Training and Orientation

After the hiring process, truncating the motivation to commit fraudulent acts continues through orientation, training, and on-going programs.

Orientations

Covering all aspects of asset protection in the orientation is a must. First, it lets your associates know that you are well-versed on aspects of crime and dishonesty. Secondly, it exposes them to the tools at hand so that the perception of means diminishes. Morale is important, so present associate dishonesty objectively and frankly, but do not sound as if you are charging your new hires on the spot. Make sure you cover the following topics thoroughly. Facilitate the meeting rather then lecturing so that they are involved in the thought process. Just as I try to do in this book, make sure they understand the "why" of policies as well as the policy itself:

- Explain what asset protection, shrink, and inventory are.
- Review store rules, like designated employee entrances, lockers, and associate purchases.
- Cover your check policy and credit card policy.
- Cover your merchandise return policy.
- Cover safety issues, like fire drills and reporting accidents.
- Let the associate know about camera systems, POS tracking systems, and any other tool that will dissuade them from theft.
- Explain to your associates how their commitment to these programs increases profit and with that increase they will be rewarded.

Posters/Motivational Tools

Marketing companies may descend upon you with catchy programs and colorful posters, but assess these with a measure of skepticism. Associates are inundated with media all day, and when they have a break they usually will not notice posters and signs let alone actually read them. Large corporations often buy into these programs, spending millions on attempted education. They will force involvement, but the idea of forced motivation is ironic. I have never seen any company present a compelling argument that broad media programs have a positive effect in every store. Your own creativity is just as effective and a lot less money then these organized programs. However, purchasing large simple posters for display in the stockrooms, near time clocks, or in break rooms can reinforce fundamental programs effectively without requiring an elevated level of associate interaction.

Telephone Hotlines

Some associates are uncomfortable about revealing another associate's act of defalcation. There are companies that will let you sign up as a client where associates can call an 800 number and anonymously report crimes. They are assigned a code number that allows them to collect a reward if their tip results in an arrest or dismissal. The cost for the program is nominal, but it would only be useful if you have more than ten employees.

Code of Conducts

Giving your associates clear guidelines of your expectations is important, both to create a positive working culture and to document training in case you need to dismiss them. Your expectations will include customer service standards and administrative standards, and should also include those items that can result in immediate termination:

- Gross insubordination.
- Violation of the drug-free workplace policy.

- Physical violence or threats of violence directed toward others.
- Theft of merchandise or company property.
- Deliberate damage to company property.
- Recording work times for another associate, or allowing another to punch in or out for you.
- Misuse of company cash, such as petty cash funds.
- Falsification of any record including transaction records.
- Violating discount privileges.
- Misappropriation of company resources, like making long distance phone calls on company phones that are not business related.
- Conducting a personal business that directly competes with the company (conflict of interests issues).
- Falsification of employment application.
- Conviction for criminal acts.
- Sexual, racial, or other harassment of other associates.
- Job abandonment—absence for two or more consecutive days without contacting the company.

You may have codes that you feel are of equal importance. The above have passed the rigors of human resource review—enforcing them will not get you sued and usually will not result in unemployment benefits to the terminated employee. If you add other codes, make sure you talk with your lawyer or the labor board in your state to make sure they are legal.

Alertness Awards

When an alert associate deters a theft, they should be rewarded immediately for their efforts. The small cash award will mean a lot to them and encourage other associates to follow suit. Even if the associate is not aware that they deterred a theft, reward them anyway and explain why. For instance, you may be watching a person preparing to conceal merchandise that they have removed from a hanger when an associate walks up to give them customer service. This act startles the thief and they leave the store without stealing. The associate's intent was to be helpful, but by doing her job she saved you money. Rewarding her will reinforce her motivation to service every customer. The cash award can either be a set amount or a percentage of the recovery.

AP Committees

Empowering associates with knowledge of Asset Protection (AP) can really get them to work for you in combating shrink. Committees where real training and ideas are shared can be very effective with strong leadership. The associate response team, as described in Chapter 5, is a necessity if you intend on detaining shoplifters and have no security personnel.

General Means for Dishonest Associates

Because associates work in the store environment daily, they develop a much higher comfort level than do transient shoplifters. They know you, your security personnel, the systems in place, and the programs that have been implemented. If they perceive any of these to be weak, then they perceive a means for theft. The means is any avenue that could potentially expose them to an opportunity. This would include:

- Unmonitored or cluttered receiving areas.
- Unsecured and dark stockrooms.
- A lack of POS controls concerning cash and returns.
- Use of many exits when arriving and leaving work.
- Poor training.
- A perception of unmotivated managers and supervisors.

Case by case, understanding the methods used by employees to steal from a company will help you determine the deterrents needed to limit means. The rest of this chapter is devoted to these methods and the proactive strategies that can keep these events from happening. Chapter 7, "The Internal Investigation," discusses the investigative process required to detect and resolve these cases when they occur. Many of these types of thefts are specific to a retail type business. However, the methods themselves are usually just modified for any other business that handles cash or inventory.

Cash via Straight Theft

With this type of theft, dishonest associates simply take cash without attempting to cover their tracks. This commonly occurs in retail businesses where cash is easily available. In retail businesses, associates may use *dedicated* cash drawers or *common* cash drawers, depending on the type of store.

With *dedicated drawers*, the associate signs for a drawer that has a precounted amount of change. The associate counts the cash, signing that the amount is correct, and has sole responsibility for that drawer. This works well if you have check-out registers or few employees who can keep their own register for an entire shift. The POS system would require sign-on and sign-off features so that the transactions of individual associates can be tracked. At the end of the shift, the associate counts down the drawer and signs the totals. Later, the cash, credit, and check sales of that associate are tabulated and the drawer counted again. If the tabulated amount and the counted amount are even then all is well. If the tabulated amount is less then the counted amount, the drawer has an "overage." If the counted amount is less then the tabulated amount, the drawer has a "shortage."

With *common drawers,* registers begin with a set amount of change. Many associates use the drawer through the day. While the POS register details their individual transactions, the end-day total is the total of all cash, credit, and check transactions conducted on that register. If an overage or shortage is discovered, you cannot immediately hold an associate accountable. The drawer may be returned to the cash office, or the minimum change left in the drawer and the rest of the money bagged and returned to the office.

Many sales situations demand this latter choice of systems, because employees are both salespeople and cashiers. Department stores, auto stores, apparel stores, and sporting goods stores may need the flexibility of multiple associates using the same register and cash drawer. On the other hand, hardware stores, supermarket/groceries, convenience stores, and drug stores usually have dedicated cashiers and check-out lanes, so each clerk can have their drawer without compromising efficiency.

Other businesses may have petty cash funds or collect cash for services. Regardless, these tools can be adapted to any business that handles cash.

Methods

Commonly, straight cash theft is no more creative than shoplifting. The dishonest associate simply looks for an opportunity where they feel comfortable and takes the cash. Some scenarios are often duplicated, however, and you should be familiar with them.

- Dishonest associates take cash at the registers by not ringing even-dollar sales. This is common in convenience stores where a receipt may not be given.
- Dishonest associates who do not ring a sale may not conceal the cash immediately. They will probably put the money in the drawer to remove and conceal later. Often they use "marks" to remind them of how much cash to take. These marks can be in the form of small coins, paper clips, staples, or ripped paper kept next to the register. In addition, some may just keep notes on paper or a calculator. Be very suspicious of employees who keep small calculators near a register.
- Dishonest associates use sleight-of-hand tricks to conceal cash. You must have good angles of observation to see the act. They can often carry out the act with a customer right next to them.
- Be careful of drop vaults that are located below the registers. Dishonest associates will feign making deposits and instead drop the bill in a book or magazine.

- A lot of cash theft occurs when the associate is getting change. This allows them to leave their stations, and they feel more comfortable while moving than stationary.
- In addition to stealing cash, many small businesses have been plagued by business check theft. The dishonest associate steals checks from checkbooks, usually from deep inside so that it will be a while before anyone notices the missing checks. They will cash the checks at check-cashing services where minimal identification is needed. This allows them to use an alias and makes it difficult for you to determine the identity of the thief.

Proactive Deterrents

The greatest deterrent to cash theft is controlling the movement of cash in your business. Every time the cash moves it is at risk. From the cash office (often called the vault or cash cage) to the associate to the register and back is a long walk. Additionally, there will be needs for change and cash advances.

- Dedicated drawers need to be counted by both the cash office clerk/manager and the associate. This keeps the cash office clerk from stealing overages as well as making it easier to document employee theft or training opportunities.
- Use locking cash bags. Have the associates bag all money, checks, and credit card drafts in the bag and carry the bag to the cash office. Do not allow them to carry tills—cash can fall out and it is easy for them to steal.
- Keep associate numbers confidential. Use swipe cards if possible. Spot-check terminal tapes to see if associates use other associates' numbers.
- Cash-counting areas should be observed via CCTV or directly.
- Never allow associate access to the cash office. Have a service window or other barrier.
- Track overs and shorts on over and short tracing charts when common tills are used. The O/S charts will show a pattern after time, and you will be able to discern who is stealing cash. In Table 6.1, each associate is present on the days of some shortages, but only Joe worked every time there was a shortage. He is most likely the one taking cash. This technique is discussed more in Chapter 7, "The Internal Investigation."
- Getting change is a good opportunity for the associate to steal cash. Use change slips to ensure accuracy. If possible, have a supervisor bring the change to the register instead of having the associate carry change through the store.
- Have one set path for associates to carry money bags. Never allow them to carry money bags through stock rooms or into restrooms.

Table 6.1 Over and Short Chart Example

Register: 042	March, 19XX									
Date:	1	2	3	4	5	6	7	8	9	10
Shortage	$32	$0	$0	$45	$5	$30	$0	$25	$0	$0
Assoc.										
Mary	X		X			X				X
Joe	X			X		X		X		
Linda		X	X	X	X	X			X	X

- For cash advances, your POS system may generate a cash advance receipt and automatically transfer the values from the safe to the register. Otherwise, you will need to use a tracking form so that the amounts can be reconciled.
- If an associate counts and balances the cash bags, have them count the cash and log the cash amounts before they see the tabulated totals. This way, they cannot skim the overages off the top.
- Always keep company checks secure, as if they were cash. It is common for the small business owner, trusting in their associates, to leave checks in offices where they are easily accessible. It takes little effort to convert these to cash.

Cash via Voids

The more creative, dishonest associate tries to cover their tracks when stealing cash. They know that cash shortages are easily noted and believe that by not having shortages, they can take cash unnoticed. So they simply void cash sales to balance the register.

Voids are categorized by type and character. There are two types of voids that you must consider:

- *Void During:* This void is keyed in the middle of a transaction, usually because of an uncorrectable error on the part of the ringing associate or a change of mind on the part of the customer.
- *Void After:* This void occurs directly after or within a few transactions of a sale. This could happen because the customer immediately wanted to cancel a completed sale for whatever reason, such as realizing they had the wrong color or forgot to use a coupon.

While these are the types of voids, *the characteristics* of the void are what indicate fraud.

- *Orphan Void:* This void seemingly is unconnected to any other following transaction. This means that the items rung in the voided transaction do not seem to be connected to another sale. Both Void Durings and Void Afters can be Orphan Voids if the transaction is not rerung.

- *Linked Void:* These voids are followed by transactions that compliment the voided transaction. Links can be established by merchandise or payment type if checks or credit cards are used. Whether you are looking for the link or the POS system, the search criterion is the same.

Fraud is usually indicated when an orphan void is present. If you have limited time, you should always thoroughly investigate orphan voids, but linked voids can be quickly reviewed. These combined categories explain what methods you are looking for:

- *Linked Void Durings:* GOOD. The reason linked voids are of little concern is that the voided transaction is rerung as a legitimate transaction, so a means of theft is not there. For instance, if a customer purchased a television and then realized that they left their wallet in the car, you might void during the transaction. When the customer returns, the transaction is rung again and payment made. An automated POS system will recognize that the merchandise is the same and the new transaction was rung in a reasonable time. If you manually review detail tapes, you will see that the second transaction reconciles the void.

- *Linked Void Afters:* GOOD. The same applies for linked void afters. A customer realizes that they just bought the wrong item. Rather than conduct a refund, the associate voids the transaction after the transaction is closed. The customer purchases the same item, but in a different color or style. The POS system will recognize the link. Manually, you will see the connection as well.

- *Orphan Void During:* BAD: In the case of orphan void durings, fraud can be accomplished by displaying the total, receiving the customer's cash, then voiding the sale after the customer walks away. In this scenario, the customer would receive no receipt, so this is rarely used since customers are conditioned to look for receipts. GOOD: If a payment method is rejected, such as a check or credit card, then it will appear as an orphan void during. Usually the register tape will state a decline and it will be obvious.

- *Orphan Void After:* REALLY BAD. Most void fraud will be indicated by this type of situation. The associate simply voids a sale after a customer has left. Because this creates an overage in the register, they can steal the cash without it showing as a shortage. It is rare that there is a legitimate reason for an orphan void especially after more than five transactions from the original sale. An associate with a series of these voids is highly suspect.

Deterrents

To minimize void fraud, you can adopt several programs:

- Requiring manager approval for all voids can be time-consuming depending on your customer count, but this is the most solid defense. You may want to require manager approval for void afters since they are rare. This may require a manager code or key to allow the void.
- POS-system-generated void reports should be reviewed weekly. Employees with orphan void afters should be tracked over a period of time and surveillance conducted. If you have manual systems, look over register detail tapes and assess for yourself the type of voids conducted.

Cash via Returns/Refunds

Refunding, or merchandise returns, represents a large problem both for external shrinkage and internal shrinkage. To the shoplifter, it means instant conversion of merchandise to cash. For the dishonest associate, it means the ability to take cash with what they perceive to be no apparent tracking.

Methods

Dishonest associates use refund fraud by creating false refund records and pocketing the cash. Refunds and the ability to conduct refunds are sources of loss that affect both the inventory and gross margin shrink. When we were reviewing the inventory process, remember that returns were debited against net sales and the returned item was added back to the on-hand count. Let's assume that your store has only ten pieces of merchandise, each for $10. Your booked inventory is $100. Assume you sell five items at full retail. Your net sales are $50. You have five items in stock. If an item is brought back and returned, then the net sales are debited $10. The item returns to the floor. If you did an inventory, then you would have $60 in stock and $40 in net sales for a total of $100, equal to the booked inventory. But what if an associate rings a return without the item actually reentering the store? Your net sales are again debited $10, but no merchandise is returned to stock. If you took a physical inventory, you would have only five items, $50. Your net sales are $40 for a total of $90. Since the booked inventory is $100, you now have a $10 shrink. The loss in gross margin manifests itself as a loss in inventory.

In small stores, refunds should be easy to control. Refund controls are discussed in Chapter 8, "Controlling Administrative Losses"; our goal here is to disable dishonest associates from using the refund system to gain cash or credit. By using refund records, you can track the associate activity as well as customer activity.

Proactive Deterrents

Refund Slips

A multicopy refund slip should be filled in and signed by the customer. If your POS system has the capability, print the refund information on the slip. Give the customer one copy instead of a regular receipt. Regular receipts can be manipulated to look like a sale and used for future refund scams. Attach one copy to the merchandise and hold the item at the register. The original copy should be placed with the media.

Your POS system may allow this same data to be entered electronically rather than having to fill out a form. Either way, the same distribution of copies should be made.

Refund Processing

When a return is made, the returned item should be held at the POS system with the attached return slip. This is so that you can sign the slip and look for discrepancies immediately. The reason for this is so that the associate must have an accompanying piece of merchandise for each refund. Without it, they can simply ring a refund and manually enter the price or UPC, even though no merchandise entered. They will fill the refund slip with false information and you will never know that the return was fraudulent.

Refund Follow-Up

Whether or not you implement the above program, you must follow up a sampling of returns with customer surveys. You should mail these surveys to one out of ten customers who returned merchandise. These surveys appear to be satisfaction surveys, and they can provide valuable information in this regard. However, what you are really doing is authenticating addresses and return information. If the address does not exist, then either the associate or the customer falsified the information. If the customer responds, stating that he did not return the $400 power saw, but actually returned a $5 light bulb, then an associate is falsifying the return slip and taking the cash himself. This can also be accomplished via telephone, but this is rather intrusive and most people prefer not to be bothered at home. An example of this survey is included in Appendix C.

Return Log/Return Report

An automated system can generate a return report daily with the item, ringing associate, customer information, and/or amount. You can review this to detect trends in legitimate returns, like an item that breaks easily and should be shipped back to the vendor, as well as tracking associate activity.

Credit Fraud

With the advent of the check debit card, which carries a VISA or MasterCard logo but actually debits a checking account rather that a line of credit, the incidents of associate credit fraud have skyrocketed. The methods are essentially the same used for void and return fraud. The only difference is that they ring the credit to a credit card or debit card instead of physically taking cash. In the case of the debit card, they then have cash in their account within a few days.

Since swiping a credit card is not a suspicious act in itself, it is a preferable method over the angst caused by trying to conceal cash.

Methods

- The majority of credit fraud will be accomplished via returns. The associate will ring a return transaction using false customer information, then use their card for the credit. Many times they will do this with a customer right in front of them. This way, an observer would assume that they are conducting a routine transaction and the customer just assumes they are catching up on another duty.
- Voids will be used when the associate has conducted a purchase and then later voids his purchase. This is a simple way of keeping the merchandise for free.

Deterrents

The same systems in place for protecting from voids and return-theft work well here. In addition, never let associates make purchases in their own departments. If they void a sale in their department that was rung in a different department, it will be much more obvious.

Inventory Straight Theft

Means

Dishonest employees may steal inventory when they perceive a disorderly approach to stock. They are much more apt to steal when they see cluttered receiving decks and stockrooms. If they can come and go without restriction, they will also feel that a means for theft is present.

Methods

Inventory theft by dishonest associates can range from simply shoplifting the merchandise, to shipping merchandise out illegally. In Chapter 8, "Controlling Administrative Losses," receiving and shipping is covered thoroughly and the more clever forms of theft are described.

Deterrents

The best deterrent is to make it impossible for dishonest associates to get all but the smallest items out of the store. Small does not necessarily mean inexpensive, but generally limiting their ability to exit with merchandise will quell much theft.

- Establish a single entry/exit for associates, preferably near an office. Do not let employees use any customer entrance that they wish.
- Have managers or security check and initial receipts from employee purchases. A unique stamp is more effective than an easily duplicated signature.
- In larger stores, issue the clear plastic purses for associates to use when working. This way, they can keep their personal effects with them without having an easy means of concealment. You definitely do not want associates carrying regular purses or backpacks to their workstations. Any retail supply sells these. The cost of providing associates with a cheap clear carrying bag is minimal.
- Do not allow associates to wear coats on the sales floor. If they have smocks, the smocks should be left in the store.
- Employees need to have lockers to keep their personal gear in. They also need to keep purses and backpacks in these lockers, never on the sales floor with them.
- Keep lockers near a high traffic area like the break room or your office.
- Keep associate purchases in the security office or customer service area until the associate leaves on lunch or for the day.
- Stockrooms need to be as thoroughly monitored as the sales floor. Look for "stashes," hidden piles of merchandise in awkward places, that may be the target of future theft. Make sure that associates only access stockroom areas according to their job requirements.
- Manufacturers and wholesalers have the same issues. They need to ensure proper door control and package checks.
- Salable inventory is not the only inventory at risk. Capital inventory and office supplies can also be stolen. Marking all equipment with stickers and an indelible mark is required. Equipment should be inventoried and logged upon receipt. The inventory should be reconciled semi-annually to detect theft.

Inventory Sweetheart Deals

"Sweetheart Deals" is a common name describing when dishonest associates give away merchandise to friends or family, or provide discounts to friends or family outside of the scope of their authority. Giving away inventory to anyone is an act of theft on the part of both the employee and the recipient, but the recipient can claim that they believed the employee had the right to do so. Price overrides and discounts affect Margin Shrinkage. Most companies would terminate an associate immediately for cash theft, yet there seems to be a lot of leniency with unauthorized discounts. Whether an associate steals $10 or discounts a sale $10, it is still a $10 loss and the effect on the bottom line is the same.

Methods

- Dishonest associates will have friends or family come to their register to ring the transaction. Dishonest associates may feign scanning or ringing in some of the items, or they may ring up the entire sale, then void the sale prior to completion (orphan void during). Often, the recipient has selected merchandise for the associate as well.
- Dishonest associates may override the price for friends or family. Most associates should have some authority to make small adjustments for damaged goods, but no more that 10 percent of the price. Most POS systems support either a Price-Look-Up (PLU) override, where the associate can adjust the price returned by the register for a given item, or a discount, usually on the total of the transaction.

Deterrents

- While deductions or discounts affect the gross sales, a PLU override affects the cost of inventory. So PLU overrides should only be used to adjust the retail value of merchandise when there is an error. The follow-up is that the error must be corrected, otherwise a discrepancy appears in your inventory results. This is very important if your inventory/POS system adjusts the retail value of booked inventory as it goes along.
- Require all PLU overrides to be approved by managers/supervisors. If it is a duplicate problem that cannot be resolved quickly (i.e., when the pricing computer cannot be updated), then certainly allow PLU overrides for that item without approval.
- Require associates to add any coupons to their detail bags so that you can review deductions on the detail against the coupons.
- Use PLU/Deduction Hot Sheets that require the associate to fill in their associate number, transaction number, item, deduction, or override amount, and reason for the deduction/override, especially in discretionary situations. Review these and make sure the reasons are good business decisions.
- Do not allow associates to ring friends or family themselves.
- Review PLU override reports and deduction reports if your system generates them, otherwise plan to review detail at random.

7. The Internal Investigation

We study the motivation, means, and methods of dishonest associates first and foremost to institute preventative measures in our businesses. However, there will always be some employees who are not dissuaded by our efforts and, as for external crime, we must be prepared to act swiftly and intelligently to contain those incidents. Bringing closure to these uncomfortable situations requires thorough investigation and follow-up. The same liabilities that exist for external arrests exist for internals. Additionally, the cases are often convoluted and much of the evidence is in the form of paperwork, which is confusing to potential juries.

Other decisions must be made regarding prosecution. Sometimes, civil procedures will help you recover cash losses while criminal procedures will not. A simple case may later reveal aggregate losses unknown at first. Court appearances can be lengthy and unpleasant. Unemployment hearings may result.

All of these various factors must be taken into account when disposing of an associate case.

There are six steps to developing a solid associate case:

1. Initiation,
2. Investigation/ Development,
3. Documentation,
4. Detention,
5. Interview, and
6. Disposition.

This chronological approach to the investigative process will keep your thoughts and acts organized and ensure your accuracy and clarity.

Initiation: Methods of Detection and Identification

Regardless if the method is crude or intricate, if it is not detected it will be successful. There are several ways to detect associate crime. Some of these are active ploys, others passive. Many of these detection methods are already incorporated into your proactive plans for limiting means. You must have a specific reason to open a case, such as a case opened for suspicion of refund fraud. You do not open a case because of general suspicion. You must initiate a case based on either *direct observation* or *indications and warnings*.

Direct Observation

A dishonest act may be observed directly quite by accident or as the result of active surveillance. Such an act would require immediate intervention. This may be an observed shoplift or the result of a surveillance on a specific area, such as an area where you found a stash of merchandise. It is not unusual to stumble upon a dishonest associate case by accident. Other times, you may have initiated actions based on a gut feeling. The act of looking for dishonesty does not imply that a case has been initiated. Your reason for watching someone is not an issue—that is your job. You want to avoid having a defense attorney trap you in an irrelevant conversation about your empathic abilities. There are several methods for direct observation:

Random Surveillance

If you have security personnel or the time yourself, watching the associates in general via CCTV or other covert methods can tell you a lot about their work habits. In doing so, you may stumble upon a crime in progress or suspicious activity that points toward a pending crime. Often times the surveillance of suspicious customers leads right to an employee case, especially in the instance of sweetheart deals.

Dedicated Surveillance

If you feel that motivation is present, long-term surveillance of a particular employee can be very beneficial. You can record a video of their work shift and then review it, skipping past dead periods, or maintain direct observation yourself.

Honesty Shops

In a so-called honesty shop, you set up the means for accomplishing a crime under controlled conditions. Entrapment is when you solicit a criminal act through overt means like bribery. Simply providing an opportunity to steal is not entrapment. This could be a simple ploy like leaving currency in an empty register drawer or staging expensive merchandise in the stockroom where it could be concealed. Giving an associate extra change could be an honesty shop. Conversely, "priming" a cash bag, adding extra money so that it creates an overage, can be a good test of your cash office clerk. Whatever the set up, make sure your surveillance is clear and constant. It is embarrassing to set up $50 only to have it disappear without knowing who took it. Honesty shops can be random or they can be case specific. If you have tracked an associate for many orphan void afters, you may have someone come in and make a large cash purchase to see if the associate voids the transaction. In these shops, you want to emulate as close as possible the environment and means that the associate is comfortable with.

Indications and Warnings

These cases are opened when you reasonably suspect an associate of committing dishonest acts because of specific warning signs. This could stem from O/S charts, void or PLU reports, refund tracking, detail audits, or tips from other associates.

Walk Throughs

Do not become glued behind your desk. You must walk through the stockroom, receiving, and the sales floor often. Your presence has a great influence on productivity and honesty. Checking the cracks and crevices of your store can reveal a lot. Thieves are creatures of habit, and when they find a comfort zone, they tend to stick with the same mode of operation. If you stumble upon a pile of ripped price tags, or a stash of merchandise, then nine times out of ten the suspect will return to that spot. All you have to do is watch and wait.

Data Collection

This creative approach allows you to gain valuable information under the guise of associate programs. The best example is allowing associate discounts. When an associate makes a purchase, their name or associate number should be entered into the POS system. Family should be allowed a small discount as well. Keeping the process confidential, you then track associate purchases and payment types. You end up with a list of credit card numbers associated with the employee. Let's say that an associate's mother buys an item using her debit credit card in December, receiving a 5 percent discount. Six months later, the associate decides that she desperately needs cash and takes her mother's debit card to work. She uses this credit card to process a phony refund. When you are reviewing the refund transactions, you see this suspicious refund and note in your file that the credit card number is one previously connected to the associate. One nationwide retailer has a system that they installed last year that tracks this correlation nationwide. It produced amazing results in detecting theft, until the retailer, with infinite corporate wisdom, decided to restrict associates to using cash or store-issued credit cards when receiving their discount. This crippled the application of the idea, but the idea itself is excellent.

Audits

The POS system reports or manual reports discussed in Chapter 6 will act as indicators of employee theft. They must be routinely checked and analyzed.

Confidentiality

Confidentiality is important when opening a case. Many cases will not pan out, and unduly embarrassing associates can destroy morale as well as get you sued. No one should be involved in the process, not even other managers, unless you directly require their assistance or input. Discretion is fundamental.

Remember that you may initiate a case specific to an associate or specific to a known crime. Missing cash will indicate a crime has occurred, but you would not immediately be able to identify the responsible party.

Specific Components of Initiation and Investigation/Development

Thieves are creatures of habit, and when they are successful at stealing they will follow the same mode of operation from then on out. What they do not realize is that in any business a pattern will emerge and they will be caught. They assume that if they are not caught the first time, then it must be a foolproof crime.

If you observe an associate committing an act of dishonesty, then the detention may be made, but this does not mean the investigation is over. You need to go ahead and resolve the immediate situation, however. Do not let crimes accumulate—it is not cost-effective, and in some cases it can compromise your case. It could be weeks before they choose to strike again. Arrest laws vary, but in most states you can only arrest for a misdemeanor immediately after witnessing the crime.

This "fresh pursuit" law keeps both police officers and citizens from holding an arrest over someone's head as a point of blackmail or coercion. Even a chase would require a constant effort on the part of the pursuing officer. Stopping for lunch and then later seeing a misdemeanor suspect from hours back would not allow the police to arrest. They would have to file a complaint with the District Attorney's office. It is tempting to let a small case accumulate into a felony, but you run the risk of never having a case at all. In one scenario, the investigator observed cash theft for $100 but wanted to see that amount exceed $400, the felony level in California. So he kept the video and let the associate continue, assuming he could arrest later if needed. Two weeks later, it became apparent that for whatever reason the associate was not going to steal anymore. The arrest was no longer valid for the misdemeanor, so the investigator had to file a lengthy complaint and explain to the DA why he did not arrest in the first place. The DA was not impressed that the investigator was hoping for a bigger case, nor was the business owner thrilled that the employee walked out casually instead of being arrested.

In some cases, you will need to identify the perpetrator before you further your investigation. With cash shortages for instance, you will detect the problem long before you identify the perpetrator. In simple cases, the identification and investigation are the same activity.

The following sections list the theft situations that have been discussed and highlighted:

- how the case is commonly initiated,
- how the specific suspect is identified,
- the basic steps of investigation/development, and
- the elements of cause you must show to affect an arrest.

The method of investigation will be different depending on whether the initiation was based on direct observation or on indications and warnings, so each of these situations is broken down to reflect those differences.

Investigation Pursuant to Direct Observation

In this case, the crime may be so clear as to not warrant further investigation. If time permits, though, searching for aggregate events may reveal that the associate had repeated the act at other times. "Aggregate" means to compile or gather into a whole. In the case of criminal law, aggregate crimes would mean any crimes over a period of time of the same nature. Usually, this is six months to a year, depending on the state laws. If you observed an associate ring a fake refund to her credit card, that would be direct observation of a crime. Now that you have observed a mode of operation, you could further the investigation by reviewing all of her refund transactions. Let's say you found five other refunds in the last six months also credited to her credit card. It would be a sound argument that those were also fraudulent. You could charge her with the crime you observed and the aggregate of the other crimes you had discovered. Since you can recover the credit at any time, there is no urgency to confront her immediately, and you can investigate further this direct observation. In the case of merchandise theft or cash theft, there will probably be no paper trail to establish aggregate crimes. Therefore, your investigation would end with your observation and determination of elements of cause.

Investigation Pursuant to Indications and Warnings

A case opened due to indications, on the other hand, would require substantial development. Your two goals are to research all aggregate crimes and attempt to establish direct observation. Depending on how compelling the paperwork trail is, you may not need direct observation, but it always strengthens the case. In the previous chapter we listed the common associate crimes. Here, we look at the elements of the investigation needed before moving on.

Cash via Straight Theft

Initiation

- *Direct Observation:* You must maintain constant surveillance after the cash is concealed. Many employees will lose their nerve and put the money back.
- *Indications and Warnings—Over and Shorts:* The shortages will appear when the cash is reconciled daily. Training problems usually are indicated by small shortages, under $5.
- *Identification (if required):* Using the O/S tracing chart, a pattern will emerge showing the most likely suspect(s).

Investigation/Development

- *Direct Observation:* You will need to establish the aggregate case by not only proving that the associate had access to the cash, but that it is unlikely that others had equal access. You will need to include your O/S chart as well as a record of the employee schedule in your evidence package.
- *Indications and Warnings:* You will need to conduct dedicated surveillance until you have direct observation of the commission of the crime. Very attentive live viewing is necessary. Look for the associate to leave the drawer open after a sale. Watch for subtle dropping of money to the floor. Watch for no sales and opening the drawer when no one is around. Most likely they will conceal the money in their shoe or bra or areas other than their pockets. They may place the money in their pockets, then go to the bathroom and reposition the money.
- *Elements of Cause:* You must have direct observation of the cash theft to detain. Even though the over-and-short chart is compelling, it is merely circumstantial in criminal courts.

Cash Theft via Voids

Initiation

- *Direct observation:* Same as for cash via straight theft.
- *Indications and Warnings:* As explained in Chapter 6, orphan voids are usually the sign of embezzlement. Auditing the void report or detail tape, orphan voids should be noted. They will be for cash transactions as cash is the goal. Look for associates who have statistically more voids then others. Also, consistent overages on the O/S chart can demonstrate void and return fraud: dishonest

associates typically will take $20 if the voided amount was $22, for example, causing small overages.

- *Identification (if required):* A chart similar to the O/S chart but tracking associates work schedule will reveal who was consistently present during these voids. Many dishonest associates will use other employee numbers to conduct the void, but usually in that employee's absence. Charting who was absent or on break when their number was used will focus in on the suspect.

Investigation/Development

- *Direct Observation:* Develop the aggregate case by compiling all voids that specifically adhere to the same criteria. Do not use other suspect voids whose natures are not the same as the suspect's mode of operation. Attempt to contact customers of the original transactions (if their information is available) to see if they actually did the void. Check inventory for shortages so that you can demonstrate to the court that merchandise was sold without being reconciled in inventory.
- *Indications and Warnings:* For cash voids, you will need to conduct a dedicated surveillance until you establish direct observation. As with all cash cases, the paper trail is circumstantial. Only direct observation will solidify the aggregate case. Look for transactions that are made in between customer transactions. Continue watching until the cash is concealed, as noted under cash via straight theft.
- *Elements of Cause:* You will require the same elements as cash via straight theft cases. The void itself is not sufficient proof of intent to deprive.

Cash Theft via Returns

Initiation

- *Direct Observation:* The same as cash straight and voids.
- *Indications and Warnings:* Return surveys mailed back from customers indicate that the return was not made. Large cash returns do not match sales. Fake receipt numbers are used on the return form. Statistically higher return rates appear for one associate over others.
- *Identification (if required):* Techniques for identifying cash theft via voids are the same.

Investigation/Development

- *Direct Observation:* After observing the crime, research all the returns processed by the suspected associate. Call the customers if you can. Check the receipt information and sales history for those items. Look for repeated uses of the same item number(s). Check your on-hand count against the physical count and see if the merchandise is missing.

- *Indications and Warnings:* Dedicated surveillance will be required to establish direct observation. Watch for the cash theft as described above.
- *Elements of Cause:* A consistent pattern of fraud may be sufficient for having the District Attorney subpoena bank records, and so on, but a direct observation will facilitate a solid case and recovery of the aggregate losses.

Credit Theft

Initiation

- *Direct Observation:* If you initiate the case via direct observation, then you can detain the associate after the transaction is made.
- *Indications and Warnings:* A thorough investigation can establish a paperwork trail compelling enough for conviction. Because the body of the crime is documented by their credit records, you do not need to directly observe the act. You only need to show that they gained from the falsified transactions by connecting the transaction to their credit card or account.
- *Identification (if required):* The record of credit card numbers created via employee purchases can help identify a suspect. Banks will generally not give you cardholder information, but they will confirm a cardholder's name. Techniques used in cash theft via voids and returns will also work here.

Investigation/Development

- *Direct Observation:* Compile all false refunds or voids; prove falsity by talking to customers or establishing that the information used is fraudulent. Check inventory to see if the counts are off. Look for consistencies, like the same item number and same credit card number. Establish that the associate does or could have access to the card (call the issuing bank and say you need to verify the name of the cardholder; they will require you to give the name, but they will confirm if it is correct). If the associate used other associates' numbers, establish that the other associates did not do the transaction via time punch records or interview if necessary.
- *Indications and Warnings:* The same as above, but a direct observation would be helpful, though not essential.
- *Elements of Cause:* The credit record can be compelling enough for a conviction combined with your tracking charts and employee records. A direct observation is a bonus to the case, but a thorough and detailed report is sufficient.

Inventory Straight Theft

Initiation

- *Direct Observation:* Random surveillance usually will initiate this case.
- *Indications and Warnings:* Stockroom walk-throughs may reveal stashes indicating theft. Overall, few warnings of inventory theft are available. Deterrence is essential, and constant random surveillance of stock rooms or warehouses is required.
- *Identification (if required):* Inventory theft must be established by direct observation, not unlike external shoplifting. Either a dedicated surveillance on an area or associate is conducted, or the observation is a result of random surveillance.

Investigation/Development

- *Direct Observation:* The criteria for inventory theft are the same as shoplifting, including the need to allow the associate to exit the store with the merchandise.
- *Indications and Warnings:* You will need to observe suspicious areas and obtain direct observation of the crime.
- *Elements of Cause:* The seven elements of cause for shoplifting apply to this type of theft. Do not ever stop an associate in the store if you have observed concealment. They have privilege when it comes to inventory, and the intent is not established until they exit the building.

Inventory Theft—Sweetheart Deals

Initiation

- *Direct Observation:* Usually, suspicious activity of customers will lead you to the associate when they carry a large pile of merchandise to a specific register. Look for customers who take merchandise out of one department and carry it to another. Knowing who visits associates on breaks will allow you to identify their friends and family.
- *Indications and Warnings:* PLU override reports or discount reports will indicate this type of theft. For straight give-aways, only surveillance will reveal the act.
- *Identification (if required):* The reports or surveillance will identify the suspect.

Investigation/Development

- *Direct Observation:* You can compile all overrides but unless there is a pattern revealed, for instance the use of the same credit card number, you will not be able to create an aggregate case for prosecution.

- *Indications and Warnings:* The mere presence of unauthorized markdowns can be enough to terminate, but for prosecution, you would need to acquire direct observation. In addition, the intent to deprive would have to be established solidly. This is why prosecution for small markdowns is not viable. The associate can argue that they believed it was necessary for customer service. You would have to provide extensive training documentation to offset that claim. Since you cannot witness an immediate profit on the part of the associate, intent to deprive is difficult to establish.
- *Elements of Cause:* If the associate gives away merchandise and their actions in total specifically demonstrate an intention to do so, then you can arrest. You cannot arrest in cases where they could argue that they forgot one item or accidentally missed a scan. The entirety of the act has to demonstrate intent; that is, repeated actions or the immensity of the actions dispel reasonable doubt.

Investigative Techniques

Remember that your techniques have to be both legal and compelling. It is illegal, for instance, to use covert listening devices, so you could not collect evidence in this manner and expect to use it. You would also be breaking the law and facing prosecution yourself. If the investigative technique is unusual, check with the District Attorney's office to make sure it can be used. When you dive into a mass of records and register tapes, it is very easy to become distracted by false impressions of dishonesty. Many transactions that jump out at you as unusual end up having a logical explanation. It is very important that you gather and organize as much data as possible before beginning to form any conclusions. A wrong conclusion early on will lead you on the proverbial wild goose chase and waste precious hours. Using computer spreadsheets to input and organize detailed information is an excellent tool. Patterns will emerge only out of the totality of information. Do not fixate on one single transaction until you have seen all transactions in the same picture.

Lastly, keep your case simple. The associate is not going to employ ten different techniques to steal. They will repeat the one method that they have demonstrated success with. Even if they did try once or twice a different method, you will not be able to add these to an aggregate case since you cannot establish a pattern with isolated and unobserved incidents. Concentrate on maximizing your efforts in investigating the method at hand. Tangents may reveal more suspicions, but they will not add to your case.

Documentation

You should be taking notes from the beginning; at this point, consolidating those notes and evidence into solid documentation is required. If you prosecute, this will be the foundation of your case, and it must reflect what you will say in court. This documentation begins here, but you will add to it after the interview and after deciding disposition.

When you open a case, create a folder to keep notes, reports, and evidence in. Add to this folder a copy of the associate's employment application, associated credit card numbers, current address, and other pertinent information that you will require either for the final disposition or to investigate. Creating a face sheet with all of this information is a good way to begin. It is easy to forget certain dates or events and you can never write too much down.

Report Writing

The methods of report writing in internal cases are similar to those used for external cases. In both situations, your report writing follows the same format though the depth of the investigation will determine the complexity of the report. For the purpose of example, we will use the case of Joe Clerk. In this scenario, you initiated the case due to receiving a return survey from a customer. The customer states in the survey that they did not return a ceiling fan for $300 but had exchanged a light switch for a different type. Your investigation begins by contacting the customer. The customer states that on the date of the return, he had come in to get the different switch. The customer recalls having filled out the return slip with his information, but not receiving a copy. He states that the associate did not even ring the exchange but just waved him through the line after he had selected the item he needed.

You continue your investigation by reviewing all return transactions conducted by Joe Clerk. Joe had been working at the store for only three months. You note that there are seven transactions for cash returns that are for large items ranging from $300 to $350 dollars. The stock number of the ceiling fan used on the return in question is used three other times. Additionally, a stock number of a plumbing fixture is used twice. You contact these customers and can only reach four of them. One states that he did return a ceiling fan. This was the earliest return transaction conducted by Joe Clerk. The others have similar statements as the man who responded to the return survey. Two could not be contacted.

You determine from this that the most likely mode of operation is that Joe waits for customers who are making exchanges and has them fill out the refund slips. He then keeps the refund slip and uses them to ring a fake return of either the ceiling fan or plumbing fixture, item numbers that he has obviously memorized. At some point, he steals the cash. Your investigation of aggregate incidents is complete.

Now you set up direct surveillance with a stationary camera over a POS station that you know Joe will work at the next day. You have a trusted friend or private investigator come in posing as a customer (a police officer may even do this for you based on the probable cause at hand—that officer would serve as a witness and would not investigate the complaint) who makes an exchange like the ones described above. You observe that Joe retains the return slip and does not finish processing the exchange. Later, in between transactions, Joe rings a return using the return slip that had been filled in by your undercover shopper. During another transaction, while the drawer is open, he places several bills on the shelf beneath the register. About fifteen minutes later, Joe bends down as if he is cleaning the shelves and places the cash in his sock.

Joe leaves on break a few minutes later. As he steps out of the store, you stop him and ask him back to the office. During the interview, Joe gives you back the cash. You explain to him the other transactions and he agrees that he did them. Joe writes a statement. You then have the police take him into custody.

Here is what your report might look like. The Incident Face Sheet would be filled out as with a shoplifter. The narrative for internals should, however, again refer to all involved parties, because face sheets are often disposed of by the police or district attorney's office. You should try to emulate the police format used by the department in your jurisdiction: it makes their job easier and the DA's office will be able to understand it. The contents, though, will remain basically the same. This format is a rough version of the Miller Format, used by many police departments:

ASSET PROTECTION INCIDENT REPORT NARRATIVE / CONTINUATION SHEET
NARRATIVE   CASE NO.:   PAGE 1 OF 2   SINGLE SUSPECT
Internal Investigation Report Date of Report: April 1, 1998 <u>Mentioned:</u> Suspect: Clerk, Joe D.O.B. 11-04-73 WIT: Agent, Fred (You) D.O.B. 04-15-65 WIT: Customer, Jack, D.O.B. 06-17-54 *Etc.; Listing all involved makes it easier for the reader to keep the parties straight.*

Summary:

On this date, I, Agent, Fred, acting in my capacity as Loss Prevention Investigator of Happy Store U.S.A., arrested Clerk, Joe, an employee of this store, for theft of cash in the amount of $1,800, taken from the cash register entrusted to his care, between the period of January 1, 1998, and April 1, 1998. The cash was taken unlawfully by Clerk by ringing fraudulent returns of merchandise and then taking the cash, concealing the cash on his person.

Establishes your authority and relationship to the suspect. Briefly describe your action (arrest) and the charge. Briefly describe the method of theft.

Narrative:

On March 20, I initiated an investigation of Clerk for suspected theft of cash belonging to the company. I had noted that on 03-10-98 Clerk had conducted a transaction on register 001, transaction number 2345, for a refund in the amount of $300. The register detail tape showed that the return was for a ceiling fan, stock number 123. A refund slip, filled out by the customer when making a return of merchandise, for the transaction listed Customer as the person receiving the refund. I contacted Customer via a mailed questionnaire. On 03-20-98, I received the questionnaire back from Customer. Customer wrote that he did not return a ceiling fan but had made an exchange for a light switch priced at $8. I contacted Customer via telephone and Customer stated to me that he had filled out the refund slip but did not receive a copy nor did he receive any cash.

Keep all actions in chronological order. Write simply but concisely. Explain industry-specific items, like what a refund slip is. If you contact a customer, indicate how (via telephone, mail, etc.). You can paraphrase statements of status (witness stated that he had a broken bone), but quote directly statements of guilt or intent (suspect said "I stole the money.")

I reviewed for the period of 01-01-98 to 03-20-98 all refund transactions conducted by Clerk. I discovered that four (4) cash refund transactions were for $300 each and listed the same item number as the merchandise returned. I also discovered two (2) cash refund transactions for $300 each for item number 987, a kitchen faucet. The transactions are listed as follows:

Date	Transaction No.	Item	Amount of Refund	Customer Name
01-17-98	6575	123	$300	Jones, John
02-01-98	2342	123	$300	Doe, John
02-15-98	4334	987	$300	Public, Jane
02-16-98	9766	987	$300	Doe, Jane
02-26-98	8332	123	$300	Person, A.
03-14-98	5432	123	$300	Dude, Fred

Chart multiple transactions. It is difficult to follow the chronology of several incidents without this reference.

I contacted each customer listed on the return slip via telephone. Jones, Public, Doe, and Dude each stated to me that they had not made a refund as described and that they had not received cash. In each case, they stated that they had filled out the return slip and made an exchange, receiving no copy of the return slip.

Doe and Person could not be reached.

You can lump statements together if they indicate the same status. You do not have to repeat each individual statement when it is redundant.

On today's date, I observed and recorded via CCTV Clerk at register 001. At my direction, Spy entered the store at 14:50 and told Clerk that he needed to exchange one (1) fan valued at $15 for a different color fan. I observed Clerk give Spy the return slip and observed Spy fill out the slip with his information. Then Spy went to the sale floor and selected a new fan.

Spy returned to register 001 and Clerk did no further transaction. Spy left the store with the fan. I observed Clerk place the return slip under a binder on the register shelf.

Always note how you conducted a surveillance. Reiterate from time to time that you are observing, but do not start each sentence with "I observed"—that is logically denoted.

At 15:14, I observed Clerk remove the return slip and place it in the register printer. Clerk then conducted a transaction with no customer present.

At 15:40, I observed Clerk open the cash drawer while conducting a sale. I observed Clerk remove from the cash drawer a number of U.S. bills and place those bills on the shelf below the register.

At 16:25, I observed Clerk bend down and begin to clean the register shelves. I observed that he grabbed the bills from the shelf and immediately placed them in his left sock so that they were concealed from sight.

At 16:30, Clerk left register 001 and exited the store for lunch. I stopped Clerk outside, asking him to return to my office. Clerk returned to my office without incident.

Interview:

During interview, I asked Clerk to give me the money that he had taken. Clerk removed the bills that I had observed from his left sock and handed them to me. I counted the bills noting that there were three (3) $50 bills, one (1) $100 bill, two (2) $20 bills and one (1) $10 bill. The total money recovered from Clerk was $300.

You would have been faulty to have earlier stated "I observed Clerk remove $300 from the register drawer." You could not possibly discern this from the camera view. Be careful not to break chronology by reporting something early in the report that you would not know yet.

I reviewed the register tape and the return slip from register 001. I noted that the transaction number on the return slip was 5678. I noted that the information in the customer section was that of Spy. I further noted that the slip and the transaction detail showed that the transaction was a refund for $300.

I asked Clerk if he had taken money this way before. Clerk stated "no." I then showed Clerk the list of other transactions and explained that I had contacted the customers. Clerk then stated "Yes, I did those the same way. I am sorry." Clerk wrote a written statement stating that he had taken unlawfully between $1,500 to $2,000.

The suspect's admission is not essential, but it helps to lend credence to the aggregate amount since those incidents were not observed.

Disposition:

Clerk was terminated for misappropriation. Clerk was released into the custody of Happyville Police Dept. at 17:45.

Obviously, some parts of the report cannot be written until all stages are complete. Having the report in rough draft as you go along will save you a lot of typing once the arrest is made. You do not need the associate sitting there for three hours while you stumble through a report.

Detention of Associates

This is the point where you confront the associate, much like making a stop on a shoplifter. In this case, though, the style is calm and even evasive. Most of the time when I walk up to associates I say nothing more than "can I talk to you for a moment?" and I consider this the most aggressive I would ever get when detaining an associate. The associate usually acts like they have no idea what is going on. This is fine; you are not looking for a confession on the sales floor. I have never had a confrontation with an associate when stopping them. You should not either.

When to Detain

Once you have established direct observation, processing the complaint is as simple and straightforward as a shoplifting case. The same elements of cause should be applied as long as the act stands independent of any affirmative defense. This means that no regular activity associated with the employee's daily routine or responsibility can be used to explain the crime. For instance, if employees routinely remove money from their registers and take that money to the cash office to get change, you would not want to detain them directly after they concealed money in their pocket. They may argue that they intended to get change and were simply holding it there. You may know that this is a lie, but it still presents reasonable doubt to a juror. You would want to wait until the associate exited the store before detaining to clearly establish the intent to deprive. On the other hand, if there is no activity that allows the associate to remove cash from the register, then the mere act of concealment would be enough to establish intent. You could immediately confront and interview the associate.

In cases like the credit card refunds, there is no sense or urgency—the deed is documented and the loss can be recovered at any time. Use the time to review for aggregate incidents and make the stop after you are good and ready.

When you have no direct observation and are stopping based on an aggregate picture derived from investigation, have all your notes and questions together before stopping the associate.

Authority to Detain

The same authority extended to you as a merchant concerning shoplifters extends to employees. When you have direct observation of a crime or have established the elements of cause, then you can detain associates against their will as with any arrest. In "cold" cases, or those based on reasonable belief but not necessarily complete cause, you cannot compel associates to remain with you nor stop them from leaving. The interview would be voluntary. In these cases, you would probably not have a prosecutable case regardless of their confession, so if they storm out, terminate them for insubordination or job abandonment (after two days).

Interviewing Associates

In your office, the associate will react in many ways. Some abruptly start crying. Others will crack jokes and pretend that it is a casual meeting. Some will cross their arms in derision and try to stare you down. The interview is a delicate procedure, especially if it is voluntary.

The old "John Reed" days of interrogating suspects—the classic bright spotlight and interviewing them to the point of exhaustion technique—are long gone, except in a few metropolitan police departments. It is generally ineffective and not binding in court to badger a suspect into a confession. An effective interview is solemn, but noncritical. It is open, but controlled. While investigations are an exercise of methodology, interviewing is a skill of both intellect and creativity. In larger cases, police detectives can be excellent interviewers. Sometimes a kinship with an associate can help the interview. In other cases, an objective third person may be more effective. Interview courses can last for weeks and it would not be fair to assume that you can learn to interview in a few paragraphs. With time, you will develop the empathy necessary to facilitate great interviews; in the meantime, success will be guaranteed if you are organized and have a solid case.

Conducting the Interview

Always have at least two people in the interview. One should take notes and be positioned behind and to the side of the suspect. This person does not talk, they are only a witness. You should be in front of the suspect, but not behind a desk in an authoritative stance. You want an atmosphere that creates the sense that you are meeting with peers, not in the principal's office. You or the witness should be the same sex as the suspect.

Make sure that you will be free of distractions. Turn off the phone ringer and close the door.

Interview Goals

Your primary objective in conducting an interview is simply to gain a written confession that correlates with your investigation. The second objective is to uncover incidents that you did not know about.

A confession in and of itself has little value. Simply having "the boss" or another authority figure interviewing a suspect insinuates coercion. The insinuation is that they will lose their job if they do not cooperate. Defense attorneys have little difficulty suppressing confessions or at least minimizing them. Coupled with your investigative results, however, a written confession can reinforce your aggregate investigation.

Interview Format

Because the associate is usually tense and defensive, do not start in on them right away. A few minutes of innocuous conversation has several positive effects. First, it distracts them from considering what lies and excuses they are going to use. Secondly, they will relax somewhat if they do not feel like their entire world is about to implode on them.

Some interviews can last for an hour. Others can last two minutes. Because many associates would not steal in other venues, they may carry a lot of guilt or at least a lot of anxiety. Releasing that anxiety is a natural reflex. You can facilitate that release by seeming nonjudgmental and concerned.

As you start the interview, you must commit to being a good listener but never lose control. You should be firm and direct. Speak in plurals, even if you know of only one crime. You may start out by being specific, but leave room for expansion.

Rationalization

By allowing the suspect to rationalize their act, you shift blame away from them and onto outside sources. In essence, you are adopting good parenting skills, condemning the act and not the person. Talk about their financial situation and other life challenges. Once they think that you feel for them, they are a lot more comfortable with the idea of confessing.

This may sound terribly manipulative, but you can genuinely feel for their position. People do make really bad decisions, especially when presented with undue stress. They may actually have an underlying reason for stealing that you consider mitigating enough to not press charges. Often, I will start the interview talking about their lives and problems, and a lot of time can pass before we actually get to the issue of criminal acts.

Reserving Information

If you think you know 80 percent of the truth, but want to know the remaining 20 percent of the truth, set the associate up so that they lie and then disprove that lie. Do not ask questions where you do not know the answer; if the associate senses that you are fishing, then they will stop talking. Interviewing is a process that is most effective if you continue changing the mood of the interaction. You are in a way classically conditioning the interviewee to respond the way you want. No one likes a bully, so if you are rude and aggressive from the start, they will find a defensive stance and remain there. If you are kind and thoughtful the entire time they will think that they are manipulating you. A combination of the two, perfectly timed, is the most effective way. If you gain their respect, then act upset or angry when they lie, they will quickly try to regain your respect. To work, your anger has to be righteous, though. Do not miscue and act frustrated if you are not sure of the truth because that will only empower them.

You will know quickly if you are dealing with a hard-core crook. The trick with them is to play a little dumb and let them think they have control. Their arrogance is usually their undoing, and when you suddenly shift tactics and bury them in a barrage of facts, they humble quickly. With established criminals, their lying can be pathological. At best, they will shut up when faced with a mountain of evidence, but they rarely confess. Most associates are not this entrenched, though, and will eventually come about.

Disposition of Associate Cases

With your report finished and the written statement in hand, you now have to decide what to do. In any of these cases, termination should be automatic. Whether you prosecute is a subjective decision. Consistency is important and you should stick with your guidelines. You should keep in mind that not prosecuting sends out the wrong message to the other employees. However, you need to look at the individual case and decide what is best.

Criminal Prosecution

If you decide to prosecute, be prepared for many things. The associate may not get any jail time. The charges may be plea-bargained down to lesser charges. However, the criminal court can order restitution and make it a condition of probation. This is the best guarantee that, steadily, you will get at least some money back.

Termination

Annoying as it is, employees who are terminated for theft can still apply for unemployment benefits, which you ultimately pay for. You may appeal their decision if they issue benefits and appear at a hearing. Once you establish that the reason for separation was theft, you will usually win.

Restitution

Make sure that you enforce whatever restitution agreement you have with the associate. Call if they are late and insist they follow the contract. Use small claims court for small amounts to get a court order if needed. Make sure the agreement is within the associate's means. A small payment monthly is better than none at all.

8. Controlling Administrative Losses

Fundamental to operating a successful business is instituting daily disciplines from the onset. Trying to implement new procedures after months of conditioning is very difficult. Employees can be slow to adapt to new processes. If you decide to implement a specific plan, set it up to the best of your ability so that only small modifications need to be made as you go along.

Remember that until customer service and inventory control become reflexes, they will never be successful as programs. Continual reinforcement is necessary until these disciplines are habits.

Many of these administrative controls also lend themselves to quelling theft. The disciplines of your business serve to eliminate both error and dishonest acts.

Shipping and Receiving

Your first opportunity for shrinkage presents itself before your merchandise even reaches the stockroom. The receiving dock can easily become a disorganized clutter, and clutter is a comfortable environment in which thieves can work. Something as innocuous as taking out the garbage can be an outlet for theft. A casual regard of the receiving area is like having an unmanned room full of merchandise with a door to the back alley. Your merchandise, that you paid for, will not even have a fighting chance.

Drivers can and will steal from you. If they perceive that your disciplines are not enforced, then they will take advantage of the weakness.

Loss Factors

- Drivers pilfering merchandise before delivery—this usually entails removing single items from large quantity cartons or burrowing into pallets and removing items from the middle.
- Drivers pilfering during delivery—drivers may attempt to "innocently" leave a carton or two at the back of the trailer, behind safety blankets or hand trucks.

- Drivers pilfering from the dock—unattended, some drivers may simply help themselves to whatever is lying around.
- Dishonest associates using trash or cardboard to conceal merchandise—they will then throw out the "trash" in the outside dumpster, returning after hours to pick up the loot.
- Dishonest associates shoplifting small, expensive items from the dock and smuggling them out on breaks or lunch.
- Dishonest associates working with outside accomplices to give away fake deliveries.
- Dishonest associates using delivery methods like UPS to ship fake orders to their homes or the homes of friends.
- Passersby entering an unattended dock and helping themselves.
- Associates and customers alike rummaging through the trash looking for zeroed-out merchandise to return. This would be merchandise that you threw away because you either received credit from the vendor or it is unsalable.

Proactive Strategies

- Time restraints considered, all received merchandise should be checked for accurate counts. Pallets should never be received as a single unit without being checked. Cartons of smaller items should be spot-checked often. Where there is quantity, there is theft.
- Small, expensive items should never be left on the dock. They pose a temptation for both drivers and employees. At minimum, have a caged area on the dock where these items can be stored immediately. High-value small items should be transferred directly to the stockroom and stored in secured lock-ups.
- The trash dumpster should be checked periodically. Use small trash cans in the store as often as possible.
- Cartons should be compressed and paletted. Allowing intact boxes to be taken to the dumpster enables easy concealment of larger items.
- The dock should never be left open in the absence of associates.
- Restrict drivers and installers to the dock and office area. Do not let them into the stockroom or other areas unsupervised.
- If you ship via UPS or another carrier from the dock, establish a comprehensive log that lists each addressee, their information, and applicable store document numbers, such as service orders or receipt numbers. Check this log against daily records to ensure that no false entries are made.
- If you have a customer pick-up area, ensure that only merchandise scheduled for pick-up that day is in the area. Extra mer-

chandise may be staged to be given to accomplices who pose as customers.

- Ensure that high-theft merchandise, like TVs or Nintendos, are never left near the dock doors.
- Zeroed-out merchandise should be thoroughly destroyed and spray painted bright red so that it cannot be returned for cash.

Stockrooms

Stockrooms offer the potential shoplifter or dishonest associate a perfect location to steal merchandise. Long before you open the doors for business, you need to plan an efficient stockroom layout. In general, the stockroom should in some way reflect the sales floor. Think of the stockroom as an extension of the sales floor and not as a giant closet. Merchandise that cannot be found quickly and easily by associates means merchandise that will not be sold and customers who will not be satisfied.

Loss Factors

- Associates sneak merchandise out through the perimeter doors of the stockroom.
- Dark long aisles allow for easy concealment of merchandise.
- Merchandise lost in piles or deep shelves cannot be sold in a timely manner and depreciates.
- Shoplifters may try to enter stockrooms to steal and exit via perimeter doors.

Proactive Strategies

- Keep your stockroom logically organized so that it reflects the sales floor.
- Conduct occasional counts of merchandise in the stockroom and on the sales floor. Reconcile these mini-inventories against your on-hand count and, if possible, against booked inventory minus sales.
- Have several lock-ups for small expensive items.
- Ensure that fire alarm breaker bars are on all perimeter doors. This will dissuade the associate from using them as well as alert you to an unauthorized exit.
- Make sure that your stockroom is obviously marked as such and that customers will not inadvertently wander in. Have stockroom entrances near offices or POS terminals so that they are monitored continually.

Customer Service Areas

Sometimes the beneficial programs in place intended to enhance the customer's shopping experience or that of the associates can turn on you. If you have an area dedicated for customer service, then it needs to be regulated tightly.

Loss Factors

- Dishonest associates use the layaway storage area to stash their own selections, sometimes to give away to friends or to remove themselves.
- Lost-and-found articles can be stolen. This does not directly impact your inventory, but is indicative of an associate theft problem. It also harms customer service.
- Lost and recovered credit cards, usually left behind by customers, are stolen by dishonest associates and used elsewhere. In larger stores, these associates may even purchase gift certificates or other merchandise using the stolen card.

Proactive Strategies

- Ensure that layaway merchandise is secure and reconcile your layaway records to merchandise often.
- Keep a log for all lost-and-found articles. Even though it does not affect your inventory, theft of lost-and-found articles may indicate an employee predisposed to theft.
- Log in all lost credit cards. Allow twenty-four hours for the customer to return if you cannot contact them. Then call the bank and let them know that you are destroying the card. Require two signatures on the log to indicate that the card was destroyed. Dishonest associates may steal cards left casually around, possibly even buying merchandise from you!

Payroll

Every business has a payroll, and the payroll is one of the greatest expenditures. Theft of payroll can occur when associates take extended breaks or have others clock in for them.

Loss Factors

- Employees have other employees clock in and out for them. This can easily happen in larger businesses, especially manufacturing business.
- Employees take extended breaks, which are usually not recorded.

Proactive Strategies

- Keep time clocks near high-traffic areas, preferably near main offices.
- Keep the time clock areas under camera surveillance with a sign warning associates that all activity is recorded.
- Enforcing the employee entrance rule will make employees feel as if their activities are being monitored. They will not be inclined to take extended breaks.

Processing Returned Merchandise

No one likes to see their merchandise returned. "Unselling" is not the business that we are in. A return, we hope, generates another sale and the transaction is a wash.

Some types of businesses refuse to do returns at all. At the other extreme, some will accept merchandise even when it is not from their store. Instilling in the consumer a sense of confidence about your product is important, and money-back guarantees are one means of accomplishing that.

Of course, along with the legitimate returns come a flurry of refund scams as shoplifters attempt to convert their stolen goods into cash. Between the two types of returns, you can quickly accumulate a lot of used merchandise. The average return rates for most businesses are listed in Table 8.1. Even though these returns are deducted from gross sales, they do not have to represent a loss.

Returned merchandise is either salable or unsalable. If the item is defective or damaged, the benefit is that most likely you can return it to the vendor. If it is simply used, you may have to mark down the item and sell it at a discount. In some cases, depending on the gross mar-

Table 8.1   Return Rates as Percent of Gross Sales

Automotive	13.5%	Home Center, Hardware	4.0%
Books, Magazines	2.0%	Jewelry	8.0%
Cards, Novelties	0.5%	Liquor	1.0%
Camera, Catalog	11.0%	Manufacturing	N/A
Computers, Software	8.5%	Men's Apparel	6.0%
Consumer Electronics	11.0%	Optical	1.0%
Convenience Stores	0.5%	Other Apparel	6.5%
Department Stores	11.5%	Music and Video	2.0%
Discount Stores	4.5%	Service Businesses	N/A
Drug Stores	0.5%	Shoes	2.5%
Furnishings	11.0%	Sporting Goods	10.0%
Furniture	14.0%	Toys and Hobbies	3.5%
Grocery	1.5%	Women's Apparel	11.5%

gin of a particular item, it is not worth selling the item at a significant markdown. For instance, if an item cost you $20 and you are selling it for $60 retail, marking it below $40 would not net you a higher profit than if you threw it away and sold a new one. If it is a slow moving item, then certainly mark it down so you can recover some of the loss. If it is in demand and has a high margin, calculate whether or not you will make more money getting rid of the damaged item and selling the customer a brand-new one.

Loss Factors

- Returned merchandise collects and is not processed for credit.
- Some customers "borrow" specialty clothing or tools and then bring them back.
- Refunders can make a living purchasing items at one store for a lesser price, then returning them to another at a higher price.
- Refunds onto debit cards are a popular ploy for dishonest associates.
- Refunds are usually the greatest source of stress at the POS.

Proactive Strategies

- Establish a method for tracking refunders, with some sort of return form or at the POS system. This will allow you to stem the tide of fraudulent refunds as well as avoid becoming a free rental center for the chronically cheap. Have on hand forms that allow for the tracing of refunds. You have every right to ask for identification. Organize and reconcile these against the register tape on a periodic basis.
- RTVs (Return to Vendor) items should be processed weekly. Have some bright fluorescent stickers made that you can immediately affix to merchandise that is damaged, with the date clearly shown. Know the return policy with all of your vendors and be insistent about them following their policies.
- Make sure that your refund policy, whatever you choose that to be, is displayed conspicuously. Print this on the receipts if you have that ability.
- Manually, or through the POS, log large or expensive purchases by customer name. This is a great control procedure as well as being conducive to customer service.
- If you find that you are developing a problem with specific items being returned, be clever. Mark the boxes with small, colored stickers or a stamp that will go unnoticed. If you see a return for that item in which the customer insists he bought it last week, but you don't see the mark and you implemented this return control program three months ago, you can justifiably send the customer away.

Housekeeping

Janitorial services often seem to have the run of the store in early mornings. For all the effort put into watching associates and customers, no one seems to want to wake up at 4:00 A.M. to keep an eye on the custodial crew. The fact is they are just as prone to theft as anyone. Surveillance of the housekeepers is an important strategy.

Loss Factors

- Housekeeping has the run of the facility. They have an excuse to be everywhere. They have bins, carts, and equipment that can conceal merchandise.

Proactive Strategies

- Housekeepers should be locked in the building if they are working before or after regular business hours. This does not preclude safety concerns—only do this if your building has many fire exit doors. Breaks should be taken in groups, not individually. Having everyone take their breaks and meals at the same time keeps them from having the privacy that they would need to steal. One exit and entrance should be used, where equipment is checked.
- Conduct random surveillance of housekeeping at least once a week. Set up high-value merchandise in areas that you can observe. You will be surprised at how many cannot resist the temptation.
- Do not allow the housekeepers to take the trash out of the building. It should remain in carts or dumpsters for disposal later.
- Check the janitorial closets for merchandise often. Occasionally conduct surveillance in the janitorial rooms using covert cameras or a camcorder concealed in a box.

9. Tools of the Trade

Whether you are consulting, the owner/manager, or employed as the loss prevention director, the temptation to drain your capital account purchasing spy cameras hidden in smoke detectors is hard to resist. There has been an explosion in the development of new systems for asset protection and a continual refinement of old ones. However, just as you cannot specifically quantify the sources of shrinkage or the impact of shrinkage programs, you cannot show an absolute return on investment when it comes to equipment and personnel. A sales pitch such as "this is the most popular item we sell" should not motivate you to jump on board and write a check. Trends in usage of such systems swing from one extreme to the other, but shrinkage percentages tend to remain constant.

Employing a shrinkage system in one area usually drives theft into another, so while the shrinkage dollars plummet in one department, they raise proportionality in the next department. Recognizing a problem with fitting room theft in the women's department of one particular store, we utilized fitting room attendants to drive the theft out onto the floor. Then our shoplifting agents concentrated on those high shrinkage areas. This had the desired effect: shrinkage dropped in the popular sections we had targeted, but it rose in areas of the women's department that were not targeted. Blanket programs, like using Electronic Article Surveillance (EAS) on all tapes and records in a record outlet, tends to force the thieves into different modes of operation; in short, they adapt.

This does not mean that these systems and tools are unworthy. They just have to be used with calculated logic. If you could only afford to ink-tag Levi jeans, for instance, and that caused the theft of store-brand jeans to increase, the return is still greater than allowing Levi's to be stolen. Levi's have a small margin while most store-brand clothing has high gross margins. You would rather lose ten of the store brands then ten of the Levi's.

It is in the security professional's nature to love electronic toys, but we also have the background to temper our impulses. The store owners or managers, however, may range from dissenting, to supporting any equipment purchases, to a vivacious lust for every bell and whistle available. Both extremes are unreasonable: excluding all possibilities is ignorant and including all possibilities is desperate. In the long run, you will gain more mileage by limiting spending sprees and regulating the growth of your systems. As much as we can, we want to gauge the effectiveness of individual investments, and that is impossible with overlapping purchases. Security equipment acquisition should be progressive and well considered, allowing for time to measure the effectiveness of each platform.

This summary of different systems reviews various types of equipment, practical applications, and tips. The final notation lists its importance as high-medium-low, and the types of stores in which they would best apply.

Alarm Systems

Burglar alarms are an absolute necessity for any business or office. While you can build your own system from kits sold in hardware stores, the prices for monitoring and installation from most major alarm service companies are competitive and worth the money.

Equipment

There are hundreds of alarm systems available of varying complexity. They all can consist of these simple components:

- *Perimeter Sensors:* Usually in the form of magnetic sensors, these sensors are mounted on doors and windows. When the magnetic seal is broken, a relay closes a circuit indicating a tripped alarm. Some perimeter sensors are "seismic"; they react to vibrations, such as those caused by a shattered window.
- *Infrared Sensors:* These sensors are usually used indoors and react to contrasts in ambient temperatures of a room. Body heat triggers the alarm.
- *Motion Detectors:* These interior sensors are triggered when movement is detected. The motion itself creates sonic waves detected by the sensor.
- *Control Panel:* One or more of these are located near the employee entrances. They have a touch pad for arming and disarming the system, in addition to diagnostic and testing functions.
- *Audible Alarms:* Most burglar alarms will result in an audible alarm, nothing more than blaring loud speakers. Most are mounted in a protective box so that wires cannot be cut.
- *Communications Relay:* Somewhere in the building there will be a dedicated phone line connected to a relay that feeds data to the monitoring station.

- *Silent Panic Buttons:* Used as a reaction to armed robbery, these switches trigger a silent alarm to the monitoring company or directly to the police in high-risk establishments such as banks or jewelry stores.

Practical Applications

Unless you own a building full of dirt, every business needs to invest in a good alarm system.

Tips

- A good system should utilize both interior and perimeter devices. The layout would be designed to detect intruders entering the store as well as those who may have hidden in the store until after hours.
- Motion detectors should also be placed in ceiling areas and near skylights.
- The alarm system should have a control panel near the entrance used by opening and closing staff. No motion detector should be in this area since this panel would allow a period of time to enter and disarm the system. A main panel and relay boxes should be positioned far enough away from the control panel so that no one could run from the control to the relays and cut the phone wire before the time expired for disarming. A good system will note the loss of a phone line and that will trigger the alarm.
- A monitoring company should monitor twenty-four hours and dispatch police or private security as required.

Priority
High

Applicability
All business types

Camera Systems

Cameras can be a great investment, but you need to decide what you are using them for. Cameras have three general uses:

- *Deterrent:* Their presence can deter shoplifting and employee theft.
- *Identification:* These passive cameras would continually record to identify armed robbers or to watch prime areas in case something happened that required review.
- *Detection:* These cameras would actively be used to detect shoplifters or employee theft.

Equipment

- *Simulated Cameras:* These dummy cameras are meant to scare away the shoplifters, but the smart ones can tell that they are fake and the dumb ones do not notice them.
- *Stationary Cameras:* These cameras are inexpensive and can face only one direction. Their focal range can be adjusted by changing lenses.
- *PTZ Domes:* Pan/Tilt/Zoom cameras have full range of motion and zoom capability. They are usually housed in smoke-colored Plexiglass domes so that their motion cannot be seen from the floor.
- *Covert Cameras:* These small cameras, which are sometimes the size of a credit card, can be hidden just about anywhere. Some come already imbedded in fake smoke detectors or signs.
- *Camcorders:* A great resource for recording activity in a short period of time where power supplies are not accessible.
- *VCRs:* In conjunction with your camera systems, you can use either time-lapse video cassette recorders, which can record up to twenty-four hours, or continuous VCRs, which record in a normal mode. Time lapse can be ineffective for many situations, since the image is usually blurred and activity is stratified too much to detect subtle thefts. Regular continual VCRs require the tapes to be changed often unless they can be programmed to rewind and rerecord.
- *Multiplexers:* These devices allow a number of cameras to be viewed on a single screen as well as be recorded onto a single time-lapse VCR. For general use, these are a cost-saving investment; for full usage, however, they should be a part of your system but not the entire system. The pictures recorded are blurry and, depending on the number of cameras, a snap shot of each camera view can be recorded only every six to ten seconds. This is a long interval when detecting fraudulent behavior. Multiplexers usually support cameras in groups of eight, ranging up to thirty-two cameras for most systems.

Practical Applications

- Cameras over POS stations will deter employee theft, but only if the employee believes that the tapes are reviewed consistently. They are more reliable as a tool for detection once you have identified a problem. Having cameras in place allows you to immediately begin surveillance. They can be mounted visibly directly overhead or behind two-way mirror ceiling tiles for a more aesthetic look. If you cannot initially afford cameras over every register, at the minimum, place the two-way mirrors above every register. Your employees will assume that they all have cameras behind them.

- Cameras can deter armed robbers. In the case of stores at risk for robbery, a monitor should be placed on the sales floor to demonstrate that the camera system is operative. A time-lapse VCR would be required and should be set on at four or six hours. Stationary cameras would be sufficient for this purpose and color would be preferred.
- PTZ cameras are an excellent tool for monitoring associates and customers. To be effective, you must be able to afford a system that will give you 100 percent floor coverage. A partial system handicaps the efforts of security personnel, and since they prefer to sit at cameras than walk the floor, areas are neglected. Also, since you must have constant surveillance, a partial system would compromise a tight case. Further, without a crew to watch it, the investment is a waste, so you must consider personnel costs as well as the capital costs. The PTZ systems can include outside cameras. Many systems are color now, though these are still significantly more expensive than black and white. The system would include a computer processor, junction boxes, domes, cameras, monitors, and joystick/control boards.
- For specific cases, nothing is more effective then the standard compact camcorder. Since these can run on batteries, they can be placed in boxes where a small hole has been cut for the lens to see through. A good example of their use would be if you found a stash of merchandise in an unusual place on the sales floor or in the stockroom. Since many employees will set up merchandise for a future theft, you could place the camcorder so that it observed this stash. If the merchandise disappeared, simply reviewing this tape would uncover the thief. Camcorders are inexpensive and you probably own one anyway.
- Dummy cameras are really not the greatest investment. They usually look fake, and if you feel the need to use them due to cost considerations, you would be better off purchasing burned-out real cameras for pennies from security equipment companies.

Tips

- Cameras tend to clean people up both physically and on an empathic level. Anyone using cameras should first spend training time on the sales floor learning to assess people in person. Security agents who begin strictly with cameras will be less successful than those who learn to identify thieves while walking the sales floor.
- For small businesses, full PTZ systems should not be used unless you have asset protection personnel. While the cost for full systems is decreasing monthly, a quality system will still start at

around $10,000 for the basics. Each additional camera will increase the cost. Stationary cameras are fine for the smaller business. After all, what is the use of having pan, tilt, and zoom cameras if there is no one there to pan, tilt, and zoom?

- Cameras can have many technical problems. They are both mechanical and digital. They require time-consuming installation and maintenance. Deal with an established company that can guarantee the product and service. Security equipment companies come and go rapidly, so look for a company with longevity in the field. The deal that is too good to be true probably is. Invest in a camera sales company that sees you as a long-term client, not just a consumer.
- Use dark smoked domes for PTZ cameras to minimize the chance that shoppers will see the activity of the camera. Customers can be angered if they feel that they are being followed by a camera.
- Remember that camera observation is never allowed in fitting rooms or restrooms. Use of observation systems where there is an expectation of privacy can result in civil and criminal sanctions.
- Stores with long, tall aisles will find that it is much more expensive to install a comprehensive system of PTZ cameras than those stores with open sales floors, like apparel stores. No matter how flexible the camera, it still cannot see through walls of merchandise. Integrating PTZ and stationary cameras is the best approach. Use stationary cameras to observe aisles and PTZ to observe traffic areas.

Priority
High, to varying degrees

Applicability
All business types

Mirrors

Mirrors can allow you to maintain observation in otherwise blind areas, such as behind end-caps (the areas at the end of aisle shelves). They can also be an effective way to watch shoplifters if used properly. They are inexpensive and easy to install.

Equipment

- *Flat Mirrors:* These mirrors are usually installed at an angle on the perimeter walls so that you can see down one aisle while standing in another. Because they are weighted forward, strong hardware is needed to ensure that they do not fall out.

- *Convex Mirrors:* These mirrors allow for a wider view range but tend to distort the images. They are difficult to use from a distance.
- *Convex Domes:* Like the convex mirrors, these domes are placed on the ceiling to allow view from any angle. They also tend to distort the images and can be difficult to use.
- *Two-Way or See-Through Mirrors:* These mirrors are coated with a reflective film that allows you to see through them from the back side. To work, the viewing area has to be darker than the area viewed, otherwise the view is limited and activity can be seen from both sides.

Practical Applications

- If you cannot afford a camera system, a savvy security agent can master the use of angled flat mirrors to follow shoplifters.
- Convex mirrors and domes are an eye-sore; they are best used for safety purposes, such as near intersections to alert associates and customers of other people approaching.
- See-through mirrors are excellent if you have overhead offices to view the floor from. They can also be installed in the walls so that you can view the sales floor from the stockroom. Using them in place of ceiling tiles will allow you to use cameras without alerting the observed.

Tips

- Using mirrors to watch shoplifters is tricky. If you can see them, then they can see you. You must position yourself so that you can see their hands but not their face. Keep your hands busy like you are looking at stock, and they will assume you are not watching.
- If your observations for a shoplifting detention are made from the floor, the evidence is limited to your word. In these cases, recover the merchandise outside with a witness who can corroborate the recovery.
- The convex mirrors are very handy in regard to safety issues. Having them above busy intersections can alert pedestrians to the movement of others.

Priority

Medium, depending on whether cameras are available. High for industrial or warehouses where there are a number of blind intersections, especially where forklifts are used.

Applicability

Any business without camera systems.

POS Emulators (POSEM)

POS Emulators (POSEM) are computer systems that allow you to immediately observe register activity from a remote location. They can be very useful when watching for POS fraud or customer fraud.

Equipment

- *POS Remotes:* These systems can often be just another register if your registers use some form of computer screens. Ask your register supplier about systems that allow a master register to watch the transactions of other registers.
- *Computer Extracts:* Most POS computer systems will allow you to access extracts, or transaction data, a few minutes after a transaction is completed. Some will allow access to this data immediately or can display the transaction as it occurs.
- *CCTV Integrated POSEMS:* These crossover systems display current transaction activity on the CCTV monitor. This is excellent for surveillance, recording both the live action and transaction data on the video tape.

Practical Uses

The uses are many, including credit card fraud, fraudulent returns, give-aways, and sweetheart deals. Being able to remotely observe POS activity eliminates the guesswork and lengthy review of journal tape afterwards.

Tips

- POSEMS are very expensive. Even many large retailers cannot afford them. In addition, add-on systems often have language conflicts with the POS computer and can crash the entire system. Utilization should be limited to larger stores with high associate defalcation.
- POSEMS are wonderful tools, but everything they do can be done through other means with a slight time delay. Do not get roped into purchasing these systems unless you have determined a clear necessity.

Priority
Low

Applicability
High-volume stores with many associates and a demonstrated high loss due to associate dishonesty.

EAS Tags

Electronic Article Surveillance (EAS) tags are the small tags that are affixed to merchandise. They generate an active or passive signal that activates sensors at doorways if the merchandise is carried out without the tag being deactivated. They can work via magnetic, acousto-magnetic, microwave, or radio frequency signals.

Equipment

- *Disposable Tags:* These one-time use tags are usually deactivated by swiping them over an electromagnetic field. They are often added by vendors before shipping. The surface of the tagged merchandise must be smooth and hold adhesive well.
- *Reusable tags:* These heavier plastic tags are tamperproof and are removed with a tool that applies specific pressure to the two sections, allowing either a pin to slip out of a restricting hole or tabs to release. Usually, these types of EAS tags are used on clothing or any item that does not have a surface that can be adhered to.
- *Sensors:* The sensors are usually in the form of upright walls that sit on both sides of the exit. Some are in the form of long bars that are suspended above the doorway. These horizontal sensors are usually used in mall businesses where the door threshold is very wide.
- *Deactivators:* For disposable tags, the deactivator is usually a flat pad attached to the counter near the register. The pad alters or eliminates the EAS signal with electromagnetic waves. For permanent tags, the removal equipment may be hand-held, attached to the register with a cable, or countertop-mounted. Some work by applying pressure and counterpressure to specific points on the tag, others work by releasing magnetized clips with either a stronger magnet or a magnet of opposite polarity.

Practical Applications

- For high-loss stores with limited entrances, these can deter, detect, or at least slow down the shoplifters.
- For books, videos, tapes, small appliances, computers, telephones, hardware, sporting goods, and other small expensive items, the disposable tags are usually used.
- For clothing, the reusable tags are used. An initial investment will last for quite some time. Bulky reusable tags can make fitting room concealment very difficult.

Tips

- You cannot assume that someone who trips the alarm is a shoplifter, because the clerk may have not deactivated or removed the tag properly.
- Stores with multiple entrances where the registers are not near the entrance will not effectively use these systems. By the time you get to the door, the perpetrator is gone.
- False alarms are common. Most of the sensor stands have counters on them to indicate the number of times the system has been tripped. In one store, the counter recorded 560 trips in four hours.
- Merchandise within close proximity of the sensor stands can trip them.
- Many professional shoplifters long ago determined ways to bypass the system. With low-signal systems like magnetic tags, just holding the merchandise above the rack can be sufficient.
- The majority of the time, you will have no idea who set off the alarm. Most investigators in department stores think they are worthless. However, in small controlled stores, like Record/Video stores, they are a great asset.
- Disposable tags can slow thieves down while they struggle to remove them, but they are an expensive price to pay just to delay the theft. The reusable tags are much harder to remove.
- Beware of accomplice maneuvers: one will buy an item with an EAS tag and then walk out the door, with another walking out directly afterwards. The one who made the purchase carries an activated EAS tag in their pocket, thus setting off the alarm. The second has concealed merchandise, but the first takes responsibility for the alarm and reenters. They deactivate the EAS tag from his purchase, assuming that it did not deactivate properly the first time. The first person drops the EAS tag from his pocket and leaves, this time with no alarm.
- EAS tags do not circumvent the need for following the elements of cause for shoplifting. They are a deterrent and only contribute to the shoplifting elements when the exit is tightly controlled.

Priority
Medium

Applicability
Stores with single exits near registers. Benefit to Card/Gift stores, Consumer electronics, Drugstores, Record/Video, Toy and Hobby, and Shoe stores.

Ink Tags

Ink tags are like EAS tags in that they affix to merchandise. They are always reusable and are removed with special hardware. They are commonly used on clothing. Ink tags do not set off alarms. Ink capsules in the tags explode when the tag is tampered with. They are an excellent deterrent and difficult to remove. The removable tags use detachment hardware similar to that used for the reusable EAS tags.

Priority
Medium

Applicability
Clothing retailers would find this to be a good investment.

Signage

Posting signs warning shoplifters that they will be prosecuted or that they are being monitored by CCTV or plainclothes detectives can be effective if they stand out. They also can distract from the ambiance of your store. Usually, minimum signage is a good idea near restrooms and fitting rooms. Most people will not notice them, though. About 45 percent of all stores use deterrent signage. Whether or not you want to depends on the style of your store. I have added signs to high shrinkage areas and have seen no apparent effect. If you have a single trouble spot, a sign stating that the area is being recorded continuously can help. However, the shoplifter will probably just carry the item to another area.

Priority
Low

Applicability
A personal choice. If you are comfortable with them, they will not hurt, but do not expect miracles. Consider the store ambiance as well. Many of your honest clientele will not like to be reminded that they are being watched.

Secured Displays

Many high-priced items are destination items; that means that the customer came to your store specifically for that item and it would not be an impulse buy. These can be locked up safely without affecting sales. A good example of this is wall thermostats. Those easy to conceal items can cost up to $120, yet every hardware store I enter has them hanging on peg hooks on the wall. It's rare that someone would be browsing around and suddenly get the urge to buy a wall thermostat. They would buy one because they specifically needed it. Other items are also purchased with a lot of forethought, such as cameras. Having expensive cameras lying around is not going to promote sales, only shoplifters. Some items can be adequately displayed while the stock is locked up. Faucets, for instance, can be very costly, but a nice display will sell them more effectively than a stack of boxes.

Practical Application

- Lock up high-value small merchandise when it will not compromise sales.
- Helps maintain orderly and appealing displays of merchandise.

Equipment

- *Cages:* These are usually built into the display wall and consist of nothing more than hinged doors with mesh or fencelike material welded into a frame. They are ugly but effective. Usually, they are used to hold stock rather than display stock. They can be a useful, inexpensive safeguard, especially in hardware stores.
- *Glass Counters:* These are nice display cases used in jewelry stores or department stores. The cases are accessed from the employee side, and usually set up to create a corral, or against a wall with a swinging door to block entrance. You can place merchandise on top of the counters as well as inside.
- *Glass Cases:* These stand-up cases can be partial cases that enclose peg-board displays or stand-alones that can stand independently.
- *Wall-Mount Cases:* These affix directly to the wall. They are usually placed above a counter and used with peg-board displays.
- *Countertop Cases*: These stand-alone cases, the types that watches are commonly displayed in, usually revolve and can allow the customer to see many items without accessing them.
- *Lock Systems:* Most cages use simple padlocks, and cases use either sliding bolts or lever locks. Sliding locks are difficult to open, but they fall apart often and the lost piece has to be replaced. Lever locks, such as the small ones on countertop cases, can be opened with a paper clip.
- *Keyless Entry:* A new security fad is keyless systems that deactivate sensors on the glass doors. Since they do not actually lock the doors, customers inadvertently open the cases over and over, filling your

sales floor with the annoying squeal of an audible alarm. You could have a neon sign blinking "Don't Open This Door" and customers still would. Eventually, we hope, someone will upgrade this idea so that the remote control activates a locking mechanism instead.

Tips

- Use cases whenever you can without compromising your merchandising strategy (people are more likely to buy when they can touch things).
- Except for destination items, have immediate customer service available where there are locked displays. This will ensure sales and happy customers.
- Secured displays are worthless if they are not locked. That may sound elementary, but associates have a collective mental block when it comes to locking displays. Enforce this discipline from the onset, and check them often to ensure compliance.

Priority
High

Applicability
Almost any store will find a use for secured displays.

Cables/Chains

It's a sad reflection on the state of society that we have to chain down our property, but at least the manufacturers have created some decent products that are not offensive to the eyes.

Equipment

- *Retractable Cords:* These cords have spring-loaded boxes that attach to the display and high-adhesive cord ends to attach to merchandise. The retraction feature keeps your display looking nice as well as minimizes damage to the merchandise.
- *Plastic-Encased Cable:* An inexpensive tool, these cables can secure any item in place and are flexible and safe to the touch. Never use exposed cable; they can splinter and cause injuries.
- *Garment Cables:* These cables run through the arms and necks of clothing items, connecting them all together and then to the rounder (the circular displays that clothing hangs on). They must be unlocked to remove a garment, but usually are loose enough to allow the garment to be tried on.

- *Coat / Garment Locks:* These metal bars run through the sleeve of a garment and then lock directly to the rounder. They can keep merchandise from running off, but the customer cannot try the item on.
- *Chains:* Good old fashioned chain-links can secure larger items without restricting the customer from examining the item.

Practical Applications

- Retractable cords can be used for remote controls, camera displays, game equipment, telephones, and other display items. They can be broken easily, so they should be used for display items rather than to secure stock.
- Hand tools are the usual items associated with plastic-covered cable, mostly because they are unsightly and would look strange anywhere else.
- The use of garment cables are usually limited to high-end merchandise like leather jackets. These sales would warrant personal service anyway. They are a great deterrent to grab-and-run schemes as well.
- Coat locks would also be restricted to high-end items like jackets.
- Chains usually keep outside furniture in place or large items like lawnmowers. Small chains can also be used to secure display items.

Tips

- Chains can be broken easily. They deter opportunist theft, but the committed thief will not think twice about them.
- Be aware of safety hazards: long chains can cause tripping or injury if they catch someone walking by, and old cables can expose filaments of the underlying metal if the plastic sheath is deteriorating. Those little shards can really injure someone, especially children.

Priority
Medium

Applicability
Stores with expensive display items where hands-on customer service is not always available.

Drop Vaults

These vaults are installed at the POS stations, allowing associates to deposit cash as they work through the day. They cannot be opened by the associate or an armed robber.

Equipment

Drop vaults come in various sizes and shapes, but they are all built in the same fashion: a narrow slot, that is lipped inward so that the money is difficult to remove, in a metal casing with a two-key lock system.

Practical Uses

- Consistently dropping money ensures that there is less in the drawer for an armed robber or till-tapper.
- Employee theft is also deterred by having all large bills and excessive number of bills deposited.

Tips

- Do not let associates count down their drop vaults. A lot of stores allow this, but it defeats the purpose of limiting employee theft. A good system is to have two managers unlock the vaults and bag the money in bags numbered with the register number.
- Clear vaults often during heavy cash sales seasons such as the winter holidays. They can fill quickly, making it difficult to deposit.
- Check the register drawers often to make sure that associates are depositing the money and not letting it accumulate in the drawer. Be wary of those who keep large bills in the drawer.

Priority
High

Applicability
All store types.

Uniformed Guards

Many small stores have turned to uniformed guards, unarmed or armed, for their security needs. Their effectiveness is related to the size of the store: small convenience stores, for instance, could benefit from the guard, since he can observe the entire store. Large stores, like a grocery market, cannot expect uniformed guards to inhibit shoplifting—the shoplifters just avoid the guards. You may require them for other reasons; in the case of the grocery store, a lot of cash is present on the floor and in the front areas. Also, grocery stores tend to experience more gang activity than other retailers.

Tips

- Spend a lot of time looking for a reputable service. Guards are low-paid and often undereducated. Paying a little more for a good service can save you from the liability of having a want-to-be cop making poor decisions in your store.
- Armed guards are prevalent in metropolitan areas. The minimum training required by the state is not very impressive. Liability is high when a gun is involved. Research the guard company and determine the level of training. You will pay more, but if you can hire an off-duty police officer or reserve police officer, the quality and professionalism will pay for itself in the long run.
- Police the police. Security guards are no less prone to stealing from you then any other employee.
- Uniformed guards tend to distract from the happy store ambiance. Their presence enforces a stigma that the shopper is in a high-crime area or that the shopper is not trusted. If you really want the deterrence but do not want the perception, hire your own security crew and dress them in nice slacks and blazers with a professional patch on the pocket. Their appearance will not be threatening, and you will not be paying the profit margin due security companies.

Priority
Medium, depending on the type, size, and location of store.

Applicability
Convenience stores, drugstores, and groceries use this service the most. They might not be conducive to the shopping environment in other types of stores.

Plainclothes Investigators (Loss Prevention Agents)

The most experienced agents are going to come from the large department stores and nationwide drugstore chains. Even this experience is varied, though, and some of these agents can work for years without developing good discretion. As a rule, I find agents who are working toward other goals to be the most effective. College students and those putting themselves through police academies can be great employees.

Practical Applications

- Loss prevention agents are a necessity in large stores with high shoplifting activity.
- Agents can also conduct surveillance, enforce safety programs, and participate in the general business without the limitations imposed on uniformed guards.

Tips

- Unlike those in your uniformed presence, agents need to know everything that you have learned in this book, and need to be articulate and professional. They also need to be well-balanced in that they will deal with all aspects of asset protection.
- Plainclothes agents are usually paid about 50 percent more than your noncommissioned sales associates, so keep this in mind.
- Try to recruit from the large stores if you can. You can also get plainclothes agents from security services. With these, you can try them out and send them away if they do not meet your expectations.
- Many loss prevention agents (LPAs) are very professional, but some are a real liability. The "cowboy" attitude of those who want to but cannot become police officers is probably the exact trait that flushes them out of police background checks. Make sure that your LPAs understand the scope and limitations of their authority, and that they uphold the common mission to protect profits, not merely catch criminals.

Priority

High, for high-volume stores like department stores, record/video, and drugstores. Low, for small specialty stores with small floor space.

Applicability

Department stores, clothing stores, or those businesses rated with high theft should invest. Manufacturing and wholesalers have the same needs, though the agents' focus will be internal.

Merchandise Tamper Alarms

Usually used for display merchandise, tamper alarms use continuous circuits to detect when merchandise has been removed from a display.

Equipment

- *Port Strip Alarms:* These long strips have ports for six or twelve alarm systems. They usually use phone cords that end with ties, loops, or pressure switches attached to the merchandise. When any part of the circuit is interrupted, an alarm sounds.
- *RCA Boxes:* These work the same way, but use RCA plugs (the plugs commonly used as in/out jack on VCRs and stereos) in a continuous loop rather than phone cords. RCA units are usually single units.
- *Garment Alarms:* These multiport systems use coiled cables that clip to garments. If the clip is opened, the circuit is broken.
- More are being created every day.

Practical Applications

- Because they sound an audible alarm, they are better than simple cables both as a deterrent and detection method.
- Cameras, camcorders, expensive clothing, game systems, customer-use demonstrators like headphones, computers, electronics, and tools are all well-protected by these systems.

Tips

- Because these systems are easy to engineer, many companies will design a system for your specific needs at a low price.
- This is one of the few systems that can guarantee a reduction in shrinkage on specific items. It is a wise investment for larger stores.

Priority
Medium

Applicability
All larger electronic, apparel, hardware, and computer stores.

Observation Booths

Most observation booths today are leftovers from the pre-camera era, but they can still be valuable. As a floor agent many years ago, my partner and I set records for shoplift apprehensions using nothing more than observation booths. Sitting above everyone looking out through two-way mirrors we had a perfect vantage point and a wide view, something cameras cannot give you. A pair of binoculars gave us zoom capability. If you are opening a smaller store, one well-placed observation booth can be a great tool for a plainclothes agent.

Tips

- You can easily construct a booth that takes up very little sales floor space. Check your local building codes, however. There are rules you must follow or the booth will be designated a "confined space"—which means a drawer full of OSHA (Occupational Safety and Health Administration) rules.
- Make sure the door is in a stockroom so the agent can come and go freely. Make sure that the agent has quick access to the exit to make a stop.

Priority
Low

Applicability

With the advent of camera systems, very little, but a great alternative for the smaller boutique.

Fitting Room Attendants

Because of privacy laws, no one may use covert means to observe someone in a fitting room. This includes cameras, peepholes, and mirrors. The shoplifters know this, so unattended fitting rooms can be a haven for thieves. Fitting room attendants check customers in and out while keeping the fitting rooms clean. For small stores, regular associates can fill this role just by having fitting rooms locked. In larger stores, a fitting room attendant is a small investment to keep shoplifting under control. Check your fitting rooms often: if you begin to note empty hangers and ripped-off tags, consider this investment.

Priority

High, if the fitting rooms are not locked and controlled.

Applicability

Apparel and department stores.

Appendix A
Loss Prevention Strategy Worksheet

The following worksheet is designed to help you organize your response to the information provided in the previous chapters. It lists the actions that you could take, such as establishing policies or purchasing equipment, and the pros and cons of that action. From this worksheet, you will be able to set up your written strategy.

In the header section of the strategy worksheet, there are some elements that are only applicable to a new business, and others that would only apply to an established business. Filling in as much detail as possible will give you the information you need at your fingertips to prepare your strategy. Whether this supports a consultation or directly applies to your job, it is an invaluable tool for setting priorities.

Your written strategy needs to contain these elements:

1. *Assessment of Assets:* What does the business have that requires protection?
2. *Assessment of Vulnerabilities:* Looking at previous inventories and records, what assets seem to be at risk?
3. *Deterrents:* List the programs and policies that you will put in place.
4. *Indications and Warnings (I&W) Systems:* List the programs that you will use for I&W, such as audits and POS reports.
5. *Incident Response Protocol:* Establish a written protocol that directs arrest response, report standards, and prosecution standards for external and internal cases.
6. *Training Directives:* Identify training programs that you and associates will require to implement the strategies.
7. *Capital Requirements:* Identify and price capital equipment purchases, such as cameras or radios.
8. *Expansion Projections:* Identify your ideas for expansion of programs and capital purchases for the next year.

BUSINESS LOSS PREVENTION STRATEGY PLANNING GUIDE

Business Name: Prepared By: Date:

Business Type: Soft Opening Date: Hard Opening Date:

Scheduled
Inventories:

<u>ASSESSMENT OF ASSETS</u>

INVENTORY

Current Booked Inventory:

Current Gross Sales:

Estimated On-hand Inventory:

Last Reported Inventory
Shrink in Retail Dollars:

Last Reported Inventory
Shrink in Cost Dollars:

Shrinkage Percentage of
Net Profit Before Shrink:

Exposure of Inventory: ❐ Public ❐ Associates ❐ Carriers (trucks/delivery)

Top Ten Division Losses
for Period by Dollar
(Merchandise Type)

1.   Dollar Amount Lost: Percentage of Total Shrink:

2.   Dollar Amount Lost: Percentage of Total Shrink:

3.   Dollar Amount Lost: Percentage of Total Shrink:

4.   Dollar Amount Lost: Percentage of Total Shrink:

5.   Dollar Amount Lost: Percentage of Total Shrink:

6.   Dollar Amount Lost: Percentage of Total Shrink:

7.   Dollar Amount Lost: Percentage of Total Shrink:

8.   Dollar Amount Lost: Percentage of Total Shrink:

9.   Dollar Amount Lost: Percentage of Total Shrink:

10.   Dollar Amount Lost: Percentage of Total Shrink:

Average Unit Cost: Pilferage $ for Period (based on empty packaging):

Known External Inventory Recoveries: Known Internal Inventory Recoveries:

CASH

Exposure: Returned Checks Total $ for Period:

Total Shortages for Period: Percent of Bad Checks Collected:

Total Overages for Period: Charge-Backs Total $ for Period:

Percentage of Sales as Cash: Total Cash/Checks/Credit Loss $ for Period:

Percentage of Sales as Checks: Percentage of Loss to Net Profit:

Percentage of Sales as Credit Card:

CAPITAL ASSETS

Value of Land: Value of Building:

Value of Equipment:

Insured Losses for Period: Uninsured Losses for Period:

INTELLECTUAL PROPERTY

Research and Development Threats:

Other:

ASSOCIATES

Number of Managers/Executives: Number of Employees:

Average Longevity of Associates: Top/Bottom Pay (Annual):

Percentage of Employees Full-Time: Seasonal or Contract Employees:

CUSTOMERS

Average Customer Count per Day: Average Sale:

Number of Customer Accidents in Period: Number of Liability Claims for Period:

Decision	Action	Pros	Cons	Notes
❐ Yes ❐ No ❐ N/A	Shrink Reserve Established	Savings account to offset shrink effect.	Cash Flow restraint.	Reserve Percentage:

RECEIVING/OFFICE/STOCKROOM

Decision	Action	Pros	Cons	Notes
❐ Yes ❐ No ❐ N/A	Truck Audit Program	Detect thefts, shortages.	Time-consuming.	
❐ Yes ❐ No ❐ N/A	Cage for High $ Items	Controls theft.	Nominal Capital investment.	
❐ Yes ❐ No ❐ N/A	Trash Dumpster Lock	Controls theft.	None.	
❐ Yes ❐ No ❐ N/A	Carton Binders	Controls theft, keeps dock organized.	High Capital investment.	
❐ Yes ❐ No ❐ N/A	Dock Access Limited	Controls theft.	None	
❐ Yes ❐ No ❐ N/A	UPS/Shipping Log	Customer service; keeps dishonest associates from shipping stolen goods.	None	
❐ Yes ❐ No ❐ N/A	Customer Pick-up Area Controls	Controls Theft.	None	
❐ Yes ❐ No ❐ N/A	Destroyed Merchandise Plan	Controls bad returns.	None	
❐ Yes ❐ No ❐ N/A	Layaway Controls	Controls theft, customer service.	None	
❐ Yes ❐ No ❐ N/A	Building Key Controls	Tracks key issuance; ensures that building keys are accounted for.	None	
❐ Yes ❐ No ❐ N/A	Locker area for Employees	Keeps employees and personal gear in one location.	Lockers would be a medium capital investment.	
❐ Yes ❐ No ❐ N/A	Camera mounted over time clocks	Eliminates cheating from clock-in procedures.	Camera would require a small investment.	
❐ Yes ❐ No ❐ N/A	Silent Alarm wired in main cash vault	Alerts loss prevention or police to suspicious activity.	Small investment if wired to security office, otherwise part of a total alarm system.	

Decision	Action	Pros	Cons	Notes
❐ Yes ❐ No ❐ N/A	Lost-and-Found Log	Controls theft, customer service.	None	
❐ Yes ❐ No ❐ N/A	Lost Credit Card Log	Controls theft.	None	
❐ Yes ❐ No ❐ N/A	Stockroom Policies	Controls theft, heightens efficiency.	None	
❐ Yes ❐ No ❐ N/A	Mini-Inventories Scheduled	Updates on-hand count, which impacts customer service; detects thefts.	None	
❐ Yes ❐ No ❐ N/A	Lock-ups	Controls theft.	Nominal capital investment; could slow service.	
❐ Yes ❐ No ❐ N/A	Perimeter doors alarmed with breaker bars	Controls theft.	Nominal capital investment.	
❐ Yes ❐ No ❐ N/A	Stockroom entrances marked	Controls theft.	None	

RETURN POLICIES AND PROCEDURES

Decision	Action	Pros	Cons	Notes
❐ Yes ❐ No ❐ N/A	Return Slips	Controls external and internal theft; tracks customer service.	Printing costs.	
❐ Yes ❐ No ❐ N/A	Return to Vendor (RTV) program/damaged merchandise ticket	Maximum gain on vendor returns.	Printing costs.	
❐ Yes ❐ No ❐ N/A	Refund policy written	Ensures consistency; keeps customers from arguing.	None	
❐ Yes ❐ No ❐ N/A	Refund survey plan	Detects associate theft; monitors customer satisfaction.		
❐ Yes ❐ No ❐ N/A	Big Ticket Purchase customer logging	Helps with returns, good customer service, increased mailing list.	None	

EXTERNAL LOSS CONTROLS

Decision	Action	Pros	Cons	Notes
❐ Yes ❐ No ❐ N/A	Arrest Policies Posted	Minimizes Liabilities.	None	
❐ Yes ❐ No ❐ N/A	Response Protocol for Arrests written	Minimizes Liability, provides consistent guidelines.	None	

Decision	Action	Pros	Cons	Notes
❐ Yes ❐ No ❐ N/A	Response Team/ Code names	Minimizes conflict; keeps customers unaware of problems.	None	
❐ Yes ❐ No ❐ N/A	Merchandising Plan balanced with shrink concerns	Controls theft.	None	
❐ Yes ❐ No ❐ N/A	Check Acceptance Policy	Minimizes profit loss.	None	
❐ Yes ❐ No ❐ N/A	Bank verification phone numbers obtained and listed	Lowers check losses.	Some banks use 900 numbers.	
❐ Yes ❐ No ❐ N/A	Shared Information Networks	Excellent loss control.	Paid service.	
❐ Yes ❐ No ❐ N/A	Check Guarantors	100% control.	Dividend paid to company on each check.	
❐ Yes ❐ No ❐ N/A	Velocity trackers	Limits bad checks and refunders.	High Capital investment.	
❐ Yes ❐ No ❐ N/A	Credit Card Acceptance Policy	Can guarantee No charge-backs.	None	
❐ Yes ❐ No ❐ N/A	Counterfeit detection pens	No deposit losses.	None	
❐ Yes ❐ No ❐ N/A	Controlled access to bathrooms	Limits vandalism.	Can be a negative customer service issue.	
❐ Yes ❐ No ❐ N/A	Incident Face Sheet /Narrative Created	Organized and simplifies case handling.	None	
❐ Yes ❐ No ❐ N/A	Evidence locker	Keeps court evidence secure.	Fills up fast, nominal capital investment.	
❐ Yes ❐ No ❐ N/A	Civil Demand Company found	Increased income to offset LP expenses.	Premium paid to company.	
❐ Yes ❐ No ❐ N/A	Shoplift detention area established	Keeps customers and suspect safe.	None	
❐ Yes ❐ No ❐ N/A	Trespass Notices created	Limits return of criminals.	None	

Decision	Action	Pros	Cons	Notes
INTERNAL LOSS CONTROLS				
❏ Yes ❏ No ❏ N/A	Higher Pay Standard	Lowers shrink, increases sales.	Retrains cash flow; raises expenditures.	
❏ Yes ❏ No ❏ N/A	Commitment to higher full-time associates	Lowers shrink, increases sales.	Benefits are expensive; raises expenditures.	
HIRING PROCESS		Screens out undesirable candidates, which boosts customer service and sales and lowers shrink.		
❏ Yes ❏ No ❏ N/A	Past Employment Verification		None	
❏ Yes ❏ No ❏ N/A	Drug Screening		Cost involved.	
❏ Yes ❏ No ❏ N/A	Reference Checks		None	
❏ Yes ❏ No ❏ N/A	Worker's Comp Review		Cost Involved.	
❏ Yes ❏ No ❏ N/A	Education Verification		None	
❏ Yes ❏ No ❏ N/A	Credit History Checks		Cost Involved.	
❏ Yes ❏ No ❏ N/A	Multiple Interviews		None	
❏ Yes ❏ No ❏ N/A	Bonding		Insurance Premiums.	
TRAINING				
❏ Yes ❏ No ❏ N/A	Orientation Program	Emphasis at beginning lowers shrink.	None	
❏ Yes ❏ No ❏ N/A	Posters/ Motivational Tools	Can help with shrink education.	Expensive programs are unnecessary.	
❏ Yes ❏ No ❏ N/A	Telephone Hotlines	Detects employee dishonesty.	Cost involved.	

Decision	Action	Pros	Cons	Notes
❏ Yes ❏ No ❏ N/A	Code of Conduct Developed	Covers you in termination disputes.	None	
❏ Yes ❏ No ❏ N/A	Alertness Awards	Gets employees involved in fighting shrink.	Cost per award.	
❏ Yes ❏ No ❏ N/A	Asset Protection (AP) Committees	Gets employees involved.	Takes time from the work day.	

OTHER INTERNAL CONTROLS

Decision	Action	Pros	Cons	Notes
❏ Yes ❏ No ❏ N/A	Bar Code/Scanning POS	Best tool for inventory control and theft detection.	High capital investment.	
❏ Yes ❏ No ❏ N/A	Void Policies Established	Limits means for employee theft.	None	
❏ Yes ❏ No ❏ N/A	Markdown/PLU override Policies Established	Limits means for employee theft, helps control gross margin.	None	
❏ Yes ❏ No ❏ N/A	Employee entrance established	Limits theft.	None	
❏ Yes ❏ No ❏ N/A	Employee purchase controls	Limits theft.	None	
❏ Yes ❏ No ❏ N/A	Clear Purse Policy	Limits theft.	Some employees will object.	
❏ Yes ❏ No ❏ N/A	O/S charting	Detects associate theft; training issues.	None	
❏ Yes ❏ No ❏ N/A	Locking Cash Bags	Limits means for associate theft.	Cost involved.	
❏ Yes ❏ No ❏ N/A	Cash Control Policy	Limits means for associate theft.	None	

SYSTEMS

Decision	Action	Pros	Cons	Notes
❏ Yes ❏ No ❏ N/A	Burglar Alarms	Essential.	Installation and monitoring costs.	
❏ Yes ❏ No ❏ N/A	Camera Systems	Excellent tool for both external and internal loss controls.	High capital investment.	

Decision	Action	Pros	Cons	Notes
❏ Yes ❏ No ❏ N/A	Mirrors	Inexpensive way to view blind spots.	Often ugly, difficult to use.	
❏ Yes ❏ No ❏ N/A	POS Emulators	Excellent tool for detecting and investigating theft.	Very high capital investment. May conflict with current hardware.	
❏ Yes ❏ No ❏ N/A	EAS Tags	Controls shoplifting.	Expensive; often unreliable.	
❏ Yes ❏ No ❏ N/A	Ink Tags	Controls shoplifting.	Initial and upkeep investment.	
❏ Yes ❏ No ❏ N/A	Signage	Can have a small impact on theft.	Bad ambiance; not proven to help shrink.	
❏ Yes ❏ No ❏ N/A	Secured Displays	Controls theft.	Capital investment.	
❏ Yes ❏ No ❏ N/A	Cables/Chains	Controls theft.	Unsightly.	
❏ Yes ❏ No ❏ N/A	Drop Vaults	Limits robberies, theft, and internals.	Capital investment, but well worth it.	
❏ Yes ❏ No ❏ N/A	Silent Alarm Systems	Alerts authorities in critical emergencies.	Judgment call depending on your risk and the competency of the local police; costs.	
❏ Yes ❏ No ❏ N/A	Uniformed Guards	Controls losses, limits robberies.	High liability, ambiance concerns, costly.	
❏ Yes ❏ No ❏ N/A	Plainclothes Detectives	Can implement and control the entire AP program.	Cost more than regular associates; rigid screening required.	
❏ Yes ❏ No ❏ N/A	Tamper alarms	Controls theft.	None, just costs.	
❏ Yes ❏ No ❏ N/A	Observation Booths	Detects theft.	Building codes/OSHA rules make them hard to build; costs.	
❏ Yes ❏ No ❏ N/A	Fitting Room attendants	Deters theft.	Payroll costs.	

Decision	Action	Pros	Cons	Notes
TRAINING REQUIREMENTS				
❏ Yes ❏ No ❏ N/A	Incident Response—Arrest Procedures			
❏ Yes ❏ No ❏ N/A				
❏ Yes ❏ No ❏ N/A				
❏ Yes ❏ No ❏ N/A				
❏ Yes ❏ No ❏ N/A				
❏ Yes ❏ No ❏ N/A				
❏ Yes ❏ No ❏ N/A				
❏ Yes ❏ No ❏ N/A				
❏ Yes ❏ No ❏ N/A				
❏ Yes ❏ No ❏ N/A				
❏ Yes ❏ No ❏ N/A				
❏ Yes ❏ No ❏ N/A				
❏ Yes ❏ No ❏ N/A				
❏ Yes ❏ No ❏ N/A				

Appendix B
Asset Protection Report
Card by Business

This appendix lists general types of retailers and their associated risk factors. The factors are graded as either an "A" (Low), "B" (Average), or "C" (High). Manufacturers and service professionals can look at comparable retail services to draw comparisons. Also, restaurants are not listed because the variety in margins and inventory control is too broad for an effective assessment.

Remember, don't only look at your own store type. There is much to discern from the patterns that emerge when you look at the report card in its totality. This should guide you in developing your own report card, as part of the vulnerabilities assessment in your strategy. These are averages, and your business may well be one of the extremes, so let this serve as a starting point, not a conclusion.

The risk factor grades are derived from several sources, including the University of Florida's National Retail Security Surveys, published from 1994 to 1997. This report offers some interesting statistics and is a worthy source, although changes in the methodology and substance of the report require caution in analysis. I coupled this report with a phone survey of business people I know, and also tabulated statistics from my own experiences. The advantage of working for large retailers is that a department store is basically a composite of small stores and I can directly observe certain factors. The ratings reflect the average of the composite derived from these sources.

This is a general guide. While you may note that auto centers experience high check losses, you may be in a rural area with a set client base that would be insulted if you had strict acceptance policies. You must consider the uniqueness of your store when considering these ratings. Also, to better understand the implications of the ratings, consider them within the context of each type of store. For instance, while a price switching is rated as a low risk for grocery stores, you know that grocery stores usually scan bar codes that are on the package, not price tags. So that low rating means little in this context.

Key

Gross Margin	The mean percentage of difference between cost and selling (retail) price.
Shrink Reserve	The suggested shrink reserve shown as a percentage of net sales.
Shrink	
Inventory	Overall rating of shrink as a percent of net sales. There would be no way to calculate shrink as a percent of net profit in this report card because too many factors are involved. "A" is 1.4% or less, "B" is 1.5 to 2.0%, and "C" is more than 2.0%.
Cash Losses	This refers to cash shortages, usually indicating high employee theft. This can include shortages and known losses from associate cases.
Refunds	This refers to legitimate refunds. "A" is 5% or less of gross sales, "B" is 5.1% to 9.9%, and "C" is 10% or above.

INTERNALS

Frequency	Based on number of arrests made proportionate to sales dollars. The assumption would be that higher sales means more employees, but this doesn't work with high-ticket sellers, like jewelry stores. Unfortunately, it is the only data available, so we will assume the premise is adequate for most stores.
Loss $	Average loss per employee case. "A" is less than $500, "B" is $500 to $999, and "C" is $1,000 or more. Notice that you may have few associate thefts, but high losses when they do occur. Only grocery/supermarkets have low loss and frequency, because they tend to have very stringent disciplines when dealing with cash and constant supervision on the front end.

EXTERNALS

Frequency	Also based on shoplifter arrest and known thefts. Remember, this can be very arbitrary. Some stores may experience high shoplifts but not have the resources to identify and arrest thieves.
Loss $	Per incident average, "A" is $50 or less, "B" is up to $200, and "C" is $200.01 and above.
Pilferage	This refers to open or empty packages found. This can indicate high shoplift problems when it is present, but the reverse does not hold true. Jewelry stores, especially those that carry costume jewelry, do not have a problem with open packages, but the items are so easy to conceal, why would someone need to open a package? Music/video, on the other hand, has high pilferage. Because they use EAS tags in most cases, the packages are ripped open.

FRAUD

Bad Checks	Based on a formula proportionate to net sales.
Credit Cards	Based on a combination of known thefts from charge-backs and apprehensions. Don't be surprised that women's clothing is on the "C" list: professional rings almost always use women to mule or use the stolen cards.

Counterfeits	Based on a formula proportionate to net sales.
Price Switching	This is when a customer removes a price from one item and places it on another. The rating is based on number of incidents proportionate to net sales. Notice that a lot of stores rated low are those stores that scan bar codes that are part of the packaging or stores where product knowledge of the associates is presumably high.
EAS/Ink Tag Removal	This is the number of incidents of forced removal of EAS or ink tags. The formula is proportionate to net sales, though tagging programs are not consistent or influenced by net sales. Take this one as an educated guess.
Return Fraud	Based on known theft or apprehensions, proportionate to sales. This is external return fraud only and does not include associate defalcation.

VENDOR

Fraud	Known cases of fraud, proportionate to booked inventory.
Error	Errors caught by merchants in counts, proportionate to booked inventory.
Burglary	Based on an average of number of incidents for the particular type of store. Notice that high-end stores tend to be the victims, excepting discount stores, which are often in higher-crime areas.
Bomb Threats	An interesting indicator of the uniqueness of stores, this is based on number of incidents per store. Notice that larger stores with a lot of customers at any given time are usually the target—I guess threatening to blow up one or two people would not be dramatic enough.

ROBBERY

Frequency	Based on average number of armed robberies per store. It's no surprise that convenience stores are at high risk. Large, busy stores that do not operate late in the evening have the lowest risk.
Loss $	Based on the average amount of cash and merchandise stolen per incident. "A" is less than $1,000, "B" is from $1,000 to $3,000, and "C" is greater than $3,000. Note that jewelry stores, although armed robbery is rare due to tight security in high-end stores, lose an average of $35,000 per incident. A comparison between loss $ and frequency demonstrates what we all know: criminals are stupid and cowardly. The stores with high frequency usually lose little cash (convenience stores only lose an average of $100 per incident).
Violence	This rating is based on reported acts of violence in stores. Most of these acts would stem from shoplifting arrests, and since department stores, music and video stores, and grocery stores tend to use many plainclothes agents, they tend to have more fights and violence. This section offers my evaluation based on the types of shoplifters I've dealt with in these respective stores.

Asset Protection Report Card

	Apparel Children's	Apparel Women's	Apparel Men's	Auto Center Parts & Tires	Books Magazines	Camera Catalog	Cards Gifts Novelties	Computers Software
Gross Margin %	45	45	40	40	45	30	45	15
Shrink Reserve	1.5	2.0	2.0	1.5	3.5	2.0	3.5	1.0
SHRINK								
Inventory	B	B	C	A	C	B	C	A
Cash Losses	C	C	C	A	A	A	C	A
Refunds	B	C	B	C	A	C	A	B
INTERNALS								
Frequency	B	B	B	C	B	B	C	A
Loss $	C	C	B	B	A	C	C	C
SHOPLIFTERS								
Frequency	C	C	C	A	C	A	B	A
Loss $	C	B	C	B	A	B	B	C
Pilferage	A	C	A	A	A	A	B	B
FRAUD								
Bad Checks	C	C	A	C	A	A	B	B
Credit Card	A	C	A	A	A	A	A	A
Counterfeits	B	A	A	A	A	A	B	A
Price Switching	B	B	B	A	A	A	B	A
EAS/Ink Tag Removal	B	C	B	A	A	A	A	A
Return Fraud	B	B	B	A	B	A	B	A
VENDOR								
Fraud	A	A	B	A	A	A	C	B
Errors	A	A	B	A	A	A	B	A
BURGLARY								
Frequency	A	A	A	A	B	A	A	A
BOMB	A	C	B	A	A	A	A	A
ROBBERY								
Frequency	A	A	A	B	A	B	A	A
Loss $	B	B	C	B	A	A	A	C
VIOLENCE	A	A	B	A	A	A	A	A

Asset Protection Report Card

	Convenience Stores	Department Stores	Discount Stores	Drug Stores	Electronics Consumer	Furniture	Grocery Supermarket	Hardware Home Centers
Gross Margin %	30	35	30	30	30	40	18	30
Shrink Reserve	1.5	1.5	1.5	2.0	1.0	1.0	1.5	1.5
SHRINK								
Inventory	B	B	B	C	A	A	B	B
Cash Losses	C	C	A	B	A	B	A	A
Refunds	A	C	A	A	C	C	A	B
INTERNALS								
Frequency	C	B	B	B	B	A	A	B
Loss $	A	B	B	A	B	C	A	A
SHOPLIFTERS								
Frequency	C	B	B	C	A	A	C	C
Loss $	A	C	A	A	C	A	A	A
Pilferage	C	C	A	B	A	A	C	C
FRAUD								
Bad Checks	A	B	C	C	A	A	C	B
Credit Card	A	A	A	A	B	A	A	A
Counterfeits	A	A	A	C	A	A	A	A
Price Switching	A	B	A	B	A	B	A	B
EAS/Ink Tag Removal	A	B	A	A	A	A	A	A
Return Fraud	A	C	A	A	A	A	B	A
VENDOR								
Fraud	B	B	A	B	A	C	B	B
Errors	A	B	A	A	A	B	B	B
BURGLARY								
Frequency	A	A	C	A	C	B	A	A
BOMB	A	C	B	A	A	B	C	A
ROBBERY								
Frequency	C	A	C	A	A	A	B	A
Loss $	A	C	B	B	A	A	B	C
VIOLENCE	B	C	B	B	A	A	C	B

Asset Protection Report Card

	Jewelry	Liquor Wine & Beer	Music Video	Optical	Shoes	Sporting Goods	Toys & Hobbies
Gross Margin %	50	30	35	80	30	30	47
Shrink Reserve	8.0	1.0	2.0	1.0	1.0	2.0	2.5
SHRINK							
Inventory	C	A	C	A	A	C	C
Cash Losses	A	B	A	A	A	A	A
Refunds	B	A	A	A	A	C	A
INTERNALS							
Frequency	B	B	B	A	A	B	B
Loss $	C	A	B	C	C	C	B
SHOPLIFTERS							
Frequency	C	C	C	A	A	C	C
Loss $	C	A	B	A	B	B	B
Pilferage	A	A	C	A	B	A	A
FRAUD							
Bad Checks	A	A	C	A	C	C	C
Credit Card	C	C	C	A	B	A	B
Counterfeits	A	A	B	A	A	A	B
Price Switching	B	A	C	A	A	B	A
EAS/Ink Tag Removal	A	A	C	A	A	A	A
Return Fraud	A	C	C	A	A	B	B
VENDOR							
Fraud	C	C	B	A	A	B	A
Errors	B	B	A	A	A	B	B
BURGLARY							
Frequency	A	B	C	A	A	A	A
BOMB	A	A	B	A	A	A	B
ROBBERY							
Frequency	A	B	C	A	A	A	A
Loss $	C	A	A	A	C	B	A
VIOLENCE	B	B	C	A	A	B	A

Appendix C
Forms and Templates

These forms and templates can be copied and used directly, or act as models for your own form development. Customizing your forms can enhance the professional image of your loss prevention department.

Included are the following forms and templates:

- Asset Protection Incident Report
- Asset Protection Narrative/Continuation Sheet
- Notice of Trespass Form
- Preliminary Notice of Civil Demand Form
- Returned Merchandise Customer Satisfaction Survey
- Returned Merchandise Record Slip
- Over and Short Tracking Chart
- Asset Protection Incident Log

ASSET PROTECTION INCIDENT REPORT

Store:	Unit No.:	Telephone No.:

Address:

• Customer • Adult • Associate • Juvenile	Prosecuted • Yes • No	Store Case No.:

Incident Description

Date of Occurrence	Time	Report By

Last	First	MI	Alias

Street Address

City	State	ZIP	Telephone No.

Soc. Sec. No.	Place of Birth	Race	Sex : • Male • Female
D.O.B.	Height	Weight	Hair / Eyes

Clothing	Place of Employment	Identification Type	Number
Parent/Guardian	Notified Time	Release Signature	Time

	Quantity	Stock Number	Description	Price Each	Total
E					
V					
I					
D					
E					
N					
C					
E					
				Grand Total:	

Recovered/Salable $	Recovered/Unsalable $	Lost $	
Photos Taken • Yes • No	Evidence Held Released to Police	Civil Demand • Yes • No	Trespass • Yes • No

NARRATIVE	CASE NO.	PAGE _____ OF _____	• Single Suspect • Multiple Suspects

NOTICE OF TRESPASS

DATE: _____

CASE NO.:   _____

INCIDENT: _____

YOU ARE NOTIFIED THAT YOU ARE TRESPASSED FROM THE BUILDINGS AND PROPERTIES OWNED OR OCCUPIED BY THIS MERCHANT. ANY CONSENT IMPLIED TO THE PUBLIC ALLOWING ACCESS AND ENTRANCE TO THIS FACILITY IS WITHDRAWN IMMEDIATELY FROM YOU.

STATE LAW ALLOWS AN OPERATOR OF ANY ESTABLISHMENT TO TRESPASS INDIVIDUALS BASED ON ACTS OR OFFENSES THAT INTERFERE WITH THE OPERATION OF THAT ESTABLISHMENT. YOUR CONDUCT AND ACTION ON THIS DATE WAS A CRIMINAL OFFENSE.

BE ADVISED THAT YOUR PRESENCE ON THIS PROPERTY WILL BE DEEMED A CRIMINAL TRESPASS AND YOU WILL BE SUBJECT TO ARREST WITHOUT ANY FURTHER WARNING.

INDIVIDUAL: _____

DATE OF BIRTH: _____
                          • REFUSED

WITNESS: _____

WITNESS: _____

PRELIMINARY NOTICE OF CIVIL DEMAND

STORE: _____

DATE: _____

CASE NO.: _____

THIS STATE HAS PASSED A LAW ALLOWING MERCHANTS TO RECOVER CIVIL DAMAGES FROM ANY ADULT OR EMANCIPATED MINOR, OR THE LEGAL GUARDIAN (S) OF AN UNEMANCIPATED MINOR, WHEN THAT ADULT OR MINOR COMMITS THE OFFENSE OF LARCENY AGAINST A MERCHANT.

_____ STATES THAT AN INDIVIDUAL COMMITTING THE ACT OF LARCENY SHALL BE LIABLE TO THE MERCHANT FOR THE RETAIL PRICE OF THE MERCHANDISE IF IT IS NOT RECOVERED IN SALABLE CONDITION, AND PUNITIVE DAMAGES OF NO LESS THAN $50.00 OR MORE THAN $500.00.

THIS LIABILITY EXISTS UNDER STATE LAW WHETHER OR NOT THE MERCHANT CHOOSES TO PROSECUTE CRIMINALLY. CRIMINAL PENALTIES DO NOT OFFSET OR REPLACE THE LIABILITY EXPRESSED BY THIS LAW.

YOU ARE HEREBY INFORMED THAT A DEMAND MAY BE MADE UPON YOU, THE INDIVIDUAL COMMITTING THE OFFENSE, OR YOUR LEGAL GUARDIAN(S) IF YOU ARE AN UNEMANCIPATED MINOR, BY THIS MERCHANT STEMMING FROM THE OFFENSE COMMITTED ON THIS DATE. THIS IS NOT A DEMAND FOR PAYMENT BUT A COURTESY NOTICE TO INFORM YOU THAT DEMAND IS PENDING.

INDIVIDUAL: _____

LEGAL GUARDIAN: _____

WITNESS: _____

CUSTOMER REFUND SURVEY

Dear Valued Customer:

Our goal is to ensure that every customer is 100% satisfied with our merchandise and the service of our associates. We frequently ask our customers for their opinions as to the service they received so that we can continually improve.

Our records indicate that you recently returned merchandise to our store. Would you please take a few moments to share with us your experience and opinions about the transaction. We invite you to make any comments regarding our store.

Thank you for helping us provide excellent service.

Customer: Please detach here and complete. Thank you!

(logo) Store no.:   DATE OF TRANSACTION
           ITEM RETURNED/EXCHANGED

ADJUSTMENT FOR: AMOUNT RECEIVED:

TYPE OF TRANSACTION:
• CASH REFUND   • CREDIT ACCOUNT: • REPLACEMENT

CUSTOMER PLEASE COMPLETE THIS SECTION

WAS THIS TRANSACTION HANDLED AS INDICATED ABOVE?
• YES   • NO (EXPLAIN HERE)

SERVICE   • EXCELLENT   • GOOD   • FAIR   • POOR

COMMENTS

ADJUSTMENT   • SATISFACTORY   • NOT SATISFACTORY

COMMENTS

ADDITIONAL COMMENTS

PRINTED CUSTOMER NAME   DATE

STREET ADDRESS

CITY   STATE   ZIP

PLEASE REMOVE PAPER FROM ADHESIVE, FOLD AND SEAL.
NO POSTAGE REQUIRED

RETURNED MERCHANDISE RECORD SLIP			**Register Validation**

Date   Associate Number   Transaction No.

Receipt   • Yes   • No   Defective   • Yes   • No

Original Receipt No.   Date

RETURN FOR	• CASH • CREDIT CARD • IN STORE CREDIT • EXCHANGE	
Stock No.	Item Description	Price
	Minus Exchange Price:	

AMOUNT OF CREDIT/CASH DUE CUSTOMER

Manager Approval	

Customer, Please Complete This Area:

Customer Name	
Last	First	MI
Address	City	State	ZIP
Telephone No.	Reason for Return

Customer Signature:

There are hundreds of register type, so if you want your register to validate (print a copy of the transaction) on the return slip, you will have to have a printer alter the form. A three-copy form is preferred: One for the customer, one to attached to the item, and one for the audit record.

OVER AND SHORT TRACKING CHART

REGISTER NO: _____   MONTH: _____

DATE	AMOUNT												

ASSET PROTECTION INCIDENT LOG

Case No.	Date	Last Name	First	Male	Female	Adult	Juvenile	Recovery	Loss	Associate	Booked	Released	Disposition

Index